Painting

Wargaming Models

ARMOURED VEHICLES IN EUROPE, 1943–1945

I0895809

T-228615
21

Painting

Wargaming Models

ARMOURED VEHICLES IN EUROPE, 1943–1945

Andy Singleton

Pen & Sword
MILITARY
AN IMPRINT OF PEN & SWORD BOOKS LTD.
YORKSHIRE – PHILADELPHIA

First published in Great Britain in 2024 by
Pen & Sword Military
An imprint of
Pen & Sword Books Ltd
Yorkshire – Philadelphia

ISBN 978 1 39905 176 7

A CIP catalogue record for this book is available from the British Library.

Typeset in Gill Sans 12/16 by SJmagic DESIGN SERVICES, India.
Printed and bound in India by Parksons Graphics Pvt. Ltd.

Pen & Sword Books Limited incorporates the imprints of After the Battle, Atlas, Archaeology, Aviation, Discovery, Family History, Fiction, History, Maritime, Military, Military Classics, Politics, Select, Transport, True Crime, Air World, Frontline Publishing, Leo Cooper, Remember When, Seaforth Publishing, The Praetorian Press, Wharncliffe Local History, Wharncliffe Transport, Wharncliffe True Crime and White Owl.

For a complete list of Pen & Sword titles please contact

PEN & SWORD BOOKS LIMITED
George House, Units 12 & 13, Beevor Street, Off Pontefract Road,
Barnsley, South Yorkshire, S71 1HN, England
E-mail: enquiries@pen-and-sword.co.uk
Website: www.pen-and-sword.co.uk
or
PEN AND SWORD BOOKS
1950 Lawrence Road, Havertown, PA 19083, USA
E-mail: uspen-and-sword@casematepublishers.com
Website: www.penandswordbooks.com

Contents

1

Getting Started

Between the world wars, the level of technological advancement was really quite staggering. Aircraft went from canvas-covered biplanes to fast, cannon-armed aluminium monoplanes, radar entered service, machine guns became lighter and easily portable, and tanks had begun to evolve into incredibly powerful war machines.

In a similar vein, there is a huge and ever-increasing selection of hobby products on the market. The variety of products is quite overwhelming, even if you have been in the hobby for a long time. In this book, I will attempt to cut through some of the technical terminology and give a bite-sized description of what is required for a few of the most commonly used techniques. The past few years have seen the rise in the supply of contrast or speed paints by several manufacturers, although due to space considerations, I've not been able to provide guides for these.

As a solid rule of thumb, when it comes to purchasing tools, you're better off buying better quality. These may prove more expensive, but will work out cheaper in the long run, and the results will be more than worth it. It's also worth scouting the internet and asking club mates or friends for reviews to determine whether a specific tool sounds like something you would find useful and fulfils your specific tastes and needs.

Readers of other books in this series will be familiar with the following chapter, but for completeness, I've repeated it here for those new to the hobby, and have updated some of the information in line with changes in common practice.

PLASTIC, METAL OR RESIN?

The Second World War is probably the most widely supported period for models, in any and all scales, with thousands of different products available. Generally speaking, for gaming purposes these are provided in either white metal, resin, or hard and soft plastics. Recently, thermoplastic has started to appear as a material from several manufacturers: this combines the features of both metal and plastic models, although it requires assembly with superglue.

Once a rarity outside of 20mm wargaming, plastic is rapidly becoming the most common material for wargaming models. This is doubly true for vehicle kits, with a staggering number of models available in a myriad of sizes and scales. Kits range in complexity from simple wargaming kits of a few parts to high-end collectors' pieces with hundreds of components. It is easy to distinguish these by noting the manufacturer. If the kit is produced by a wargaming company, it will typically be a simple build, whereas a kit produced by a scale modelling company will be more complex. Some manufacturers, though, are starting to produce simpler kits aimed at the wargaming market. If you are in doubt, it's worth

(© *Hornby Hobbies Ltd 2023*)

checking the Scalemates website. This invaluable resource contains reviews and instructions for a vast array of kits.

Probably the most common material for the production of vehicle models in sizes smaller than 15mm, however, is lead-free metal, although kits are available in all different sizes in this material, especially amongst older or smaller ranges. Metal can be tricky to work with and can involve significant cleaning up, removing moulding lines along the sides of parts, and tidying up areas of excess metal called flash. This is a simple task and requires scraping along the line with the blunt side of a blade or a quick sanding down with some files. Again, I'll cover this a little later.

Metal models need to be assembled with superglue or equivalent. Larger models such as artillery and cavalry will require a degree of patience as they can quickly become somewhat frustrating if you try to rush putting them together. When assembling any model, patience and test fitting will always pay off.

Resin is another common material used in the production of vehicle kits. It can be found in both printed and cast varieties, although working with either is largely the same. It's also worth giving resin a wash in warm soapy water to remove any mould release agents that can hinder assembly and painting. Resin can have large casting lugs attached to parts, and these will need removing with a razor saw. Other than that, resin is much like working with metal, and requires superglue to assemble. Many kits actually combine metal and resin parts, and these can be glued together easily. It's worth pointing out that resin dust can be toxic, so it is advisable to wear a mask when sanding and filing.

At first glance, thermoplastic appears very much like a soft plastic, although it is far harder and more resilient, and not prone to bending, or flaking paint. Thermoplastic is incredibly durable. Unfortunately, this

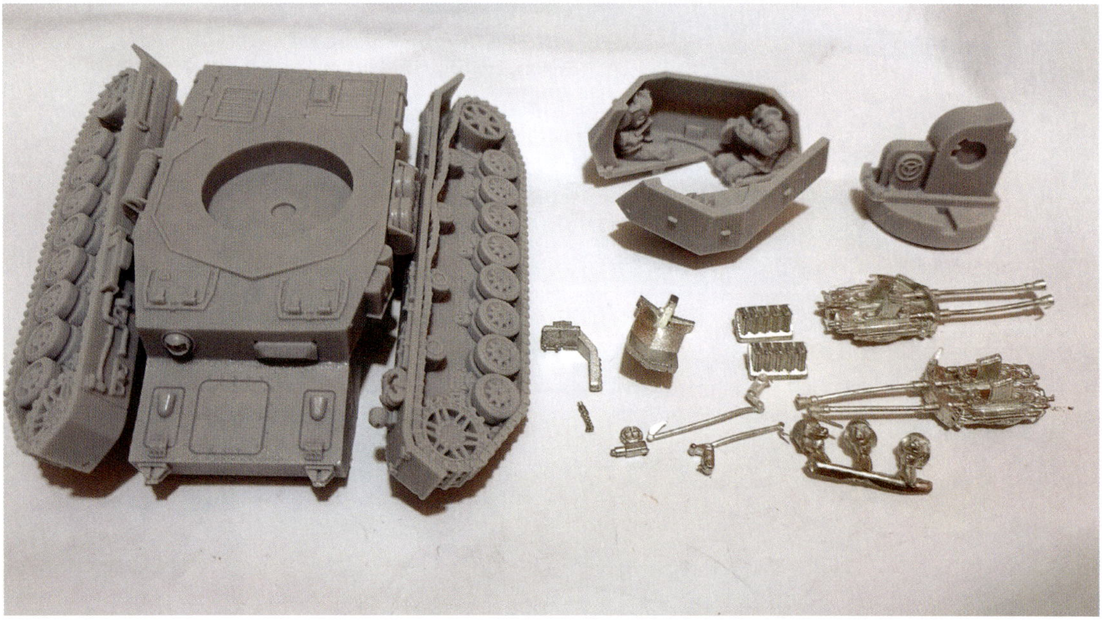

also makes the material very hard to clean up. If you attempt to remove moulding lines with a file, you will end up simply tearing the model rather than sanding the lines away. Instead, use a very sharp knife blade, and carefully clean the part up. You can also use very fine wet and dry paper, at least 1000 grit, to polish the part to a smoother finish. Thermoplastic models are a type of resin, so will not bond with normal plastic glues; you will need to use superglue.

KNIVES, CUTTERS AND FILES

The first thing you'll need to do, of course, is to get the component parts of your model ready for assembly and clean away any residue from the manufacturing process. This can take several forms, but the most common are flash and mould lines, which develop when the model is cast. These appear as either prominent lines around a part or as chunks or 'worms' of excess material, most especially on edges and undercuts of the component. These casting imperfections can appear in any material and removing them will massively improve the appearance of the finished model, especially when you are using the drybrush techniques.

HOBBY KNIFE

These broadly fall into two types: those with replaceable blades, such as the ubiquitous X-Acto hobby knife, and the Stanley knife. Either one of these will probably be your most frequently used tool in preparing your models, as the sharp side of the blade can be used for cutting things, whilst the blunt edge can be used to remove mould lines by simply scraping it down them a few times. This works, as the blunt edge is more forgiving of slips, and follows the contours of the details well.

Which type of knife you get is entirely up to you, but I'd recommend one of each, especially as they can be bought for good prices from pretty much anywhere that sells tools or hobby supplies. The replaceable nature

of the X-Acto style allows for different styles and shapes of blade to be fitted, as well as for the blade to be replaced once it becomes dull. The slender, sharp blades do have their limits, however, and can blunt quickly when working with metal. They may also struggle with cutting through thicker plastic sprues. They are very sharp, though, and give you a lot of control, especially for scraping off moulding lines or the remains of tabs after using side cutters. The Stanley knife is handy if you need to do some heavier duty cutting, such as trimming parts off for a conversion that side cutters can't perform as cleanly as you need.

SIDE CUTTERS

Also known as sprue cutters, these are vaguely similar to scissors, but with a shorter blade and more powerful, tensioned action. As the name suggests, these are good at cutting things. Perfect for removing plastic parts from their carrying sprue, it's best to trim the part leaving a small stub of plastic that you can then trim with a knife or file. Also handy for metal, these can be used for removing casting lugs or parts from moulding blocks. Sprue cutters can be found in the majority of model shops, both on and offline. I'd recommend getting maybe two sets, and

having one for metal and one for plastic if you're likely to work on a lot of both materials, as the set for metal will blunt faster than the set used on plastics.

FILES

Files are another immensely useful tool and can be purchased from most tool or hardware shops as well as model and hobby shops. Ideally, what you want is a set of jeweller's files, or needle files. These typically come in sets of several different files, with each being a different shape to allow the cleaning of most parts of a model. A file

Excess plastic is removed with a file.

with a blade more than a centimetre wide will probably prove to be too big for modelling purposes, so aim for something quite fine. These are great tools for removing mould lines and getting rid of the contact points of sprue gates.

GLUES

Now that we have established what the models are made from, and have trimmed and cleaned the parts, it's time to start sticking things together. For this, we'll need to ensure we are matching the correct bonding agent to the right material. Very broadly speaking, the most commonly encountered glues are PVA, superglue, cement and solvent.

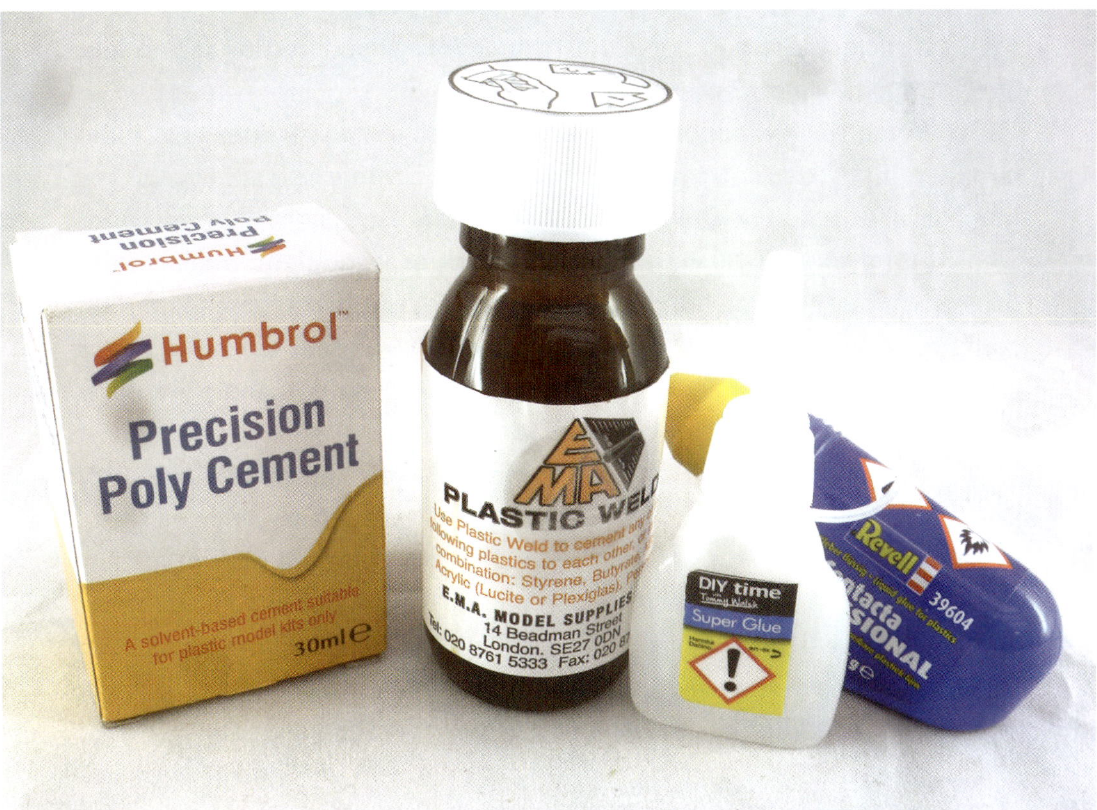

Here, glue is being applied to the join.

PVA is a sticky paste and fine for attaching foliage and netting to models, but not much use beyond that.

Superglue, or cyanoacrylate, to give it its proper name, is a rapid curing cement that bonds most materials. Given the rapidity of the bonding process, superglue works best when used in small, controlled areas. I tend to apply it with a cocktail stick or equivalent, adding small dabs to each part to be bonded. It's best to get the parts joined and then come back and carefully add more superglue if you feel the bond needs it rather than flood an area that will take forever to dry, and potentially make a terrible mess of your model, too.

Adhesives for plastics such as those from Revell, Tamiya and Humbrol are all solvent based, to varying degrees, and have a fairly wide range of drying times. In addition, there are also solvents designed with modelling in mind, such as plastic weld, which are far more potent. All of these function on the principle of partially melting the two bonding surfaces of plastic into a very strong bond. However, they won't bond metal, resin, or plastic to metal or resin. For this you will still need superglue.

Finally, we have cements. These typically come supplied in tubes and are very sticky and foul-smelling. Whilst eventually they can give a decent bond, they are for the most part inferior to the purpose-designed adhesives already mentioned and should probably be avoided.

It's also worth checking the drying times for various glues. Superglue can have an activator that will speed up the drying times for when you need an even quicker bond. Alternatively, especially when working with small parts, a more gel type glue is very good as this will hold the part in place and allow you to adjust positioning and fit.

FILLER

Gaps are something of an inevitability when working with multipart kits. Sometimes these are small and can be hidden or ignored, especially with smaller scale models, but if they are in prominent areas, they will require treatment.

If you do decide to fill the seams and gaps, then broadly speaking there are two types of filler you can use: epoxy putty and model filler. The key distinction between these is that filler comes premixed, ready to apply, usually in a tube similar to toothpaste, and epoxy putty is made by mixing two compounds together.

Here, the putty is being applied to the gap.

The excess filler is removed with a cotton bud.

Model filler is pretty easy to find in most brick and mortar hobby shops, and is widely manufactured by the likes of Humbrol, Revell, Vallejo and the like. It is very simple to use – just squeeze some onto a piece of card and then apply it with a cocktail stick to the area to be filled. Once dry, it's easily sanded with files or wet and dry paper. Most fillers take a few hours to dry before they are ready to be sanded and shaped.

Acrylic fillers, such as that produced by Vallejo, can be applied to a gap, allowed to set for forty-five minutes or so and the excess removed with a damp cotton bud, or be allowed to fully harden and then sanded with files or wet and dry paper.

PAINT AND PRIMER AND SPRAY CANS

Now that our model is built, we can start to paint it. Before we can look at some techniques, though, I should probably cover a few key types of paint and paint products on the market. Before painting, it's best practice to give your models a wash in warm soapy water to remove any

release agents, dust, finger grease etc. that can build up on the model and potentially harm the finish.

All of the following guides in this book will be for painting over primed models. For most of these I'll be using a black primer, as it provides a deep shadow colour and will speed up the painting of the model.

Firstly, primers are probably the most important type of paint you can get, especially when working with resin or metal. These differ from paint in being specially formulated to give a hardwearing coat that gives a resilient surface for handling and painting. With most paints for wargaming being water-based, this is particularly important as repeated handling without a primer can cause paint to wear off a finished model. Primers typically come in black, white, grey and dark red, and I prefer to get them from places selling car body paints.

When working with purely plastic models, you can get away with using coloured spray paints as the initial layer of colour. There are a great many of these on the market in both enamel and acrylic form, so finding something to fit your needs shouldn't be too hard. Notable ranges are The Army Painter, Citadel, Plastic Soldier Company, Tamiya and Humbrol. When working with these sprays, I'd still suggest applying a light coating of primer and allowing this to dry thoroughly (at least twelve hours, better for twenty-four, though) before applying the colour spray.

By far the most popular paints used for wargaming are acrylic. These are water-soluble, but quick-drying and hardwearing. Most paints as purchased require some thinning to get the best results, as paint that is too thick will not only be difficult to get where you want it to go, but it may also swamp the detail on your model. To thin your paint, simply apply a little paint to a pallet (an old tile or plastic lid is great for this), then add an equal amount of water and stir together using an old brush.

For best results, add a tiny amount of flow improver. This will hold the coverage of the paint together well whilst still keeping the paint

controllable. It's hard to give any ratio of paint to water as it depends on the type of paints you have, the brands, and even the colours used.

When preparing paint for airbrushing, you will need to mix it a little thinner. As a rough guide, you will want an approximately 50:50 mix of paint to thinner, although this varies between both paint range and individual paint. If your paint range has its own brand of thinner, I'd also suggest using this to mix with the paint for airbrushing rather than using pure water, as it will ensure the paint flows as intended. With airbrushing, it is always recommended to experiment on some spare plastic to get a better idea of how the paint will perform before committing to the model.

Enamel paints are an oil-based product, and whilst prevalent as paints in their own right, are now largely used for weathering effects. They have longer drying times than acrylics but allow you to work and blend them with mineral spirits.

Finally, oil paints are very useful for weathering. They can be thinned using mineral spirits or white spirit. It's recommended to use them in a well-ventilated area. They have a longer drying time than enamels and can be reactivated several days after they have been applied to a model. This makes them ideal for subtle weathering effects, as we will see later in this book.

PAINTBRUSHES AND CARE

As with most tools, brushes vary between super cheap, where you get a pack of a dozen brushes for a few pounds, up to fine Kolinsky sable brushes that can seem hugely expensive in comparison. As someone who paints a huge number of models, I find it's worth splashing out on the best quality brushes you can afford, as they will last longer and work out cheaper in the long term. To illustrate this, I've had some expensive brushes that are used pretty much every day, for long periods, which are still very functional, if a bit worn now. I also have a steady stream of cheaper brushes that seem to last a few months before being relegated to mixing and stirring purposes.

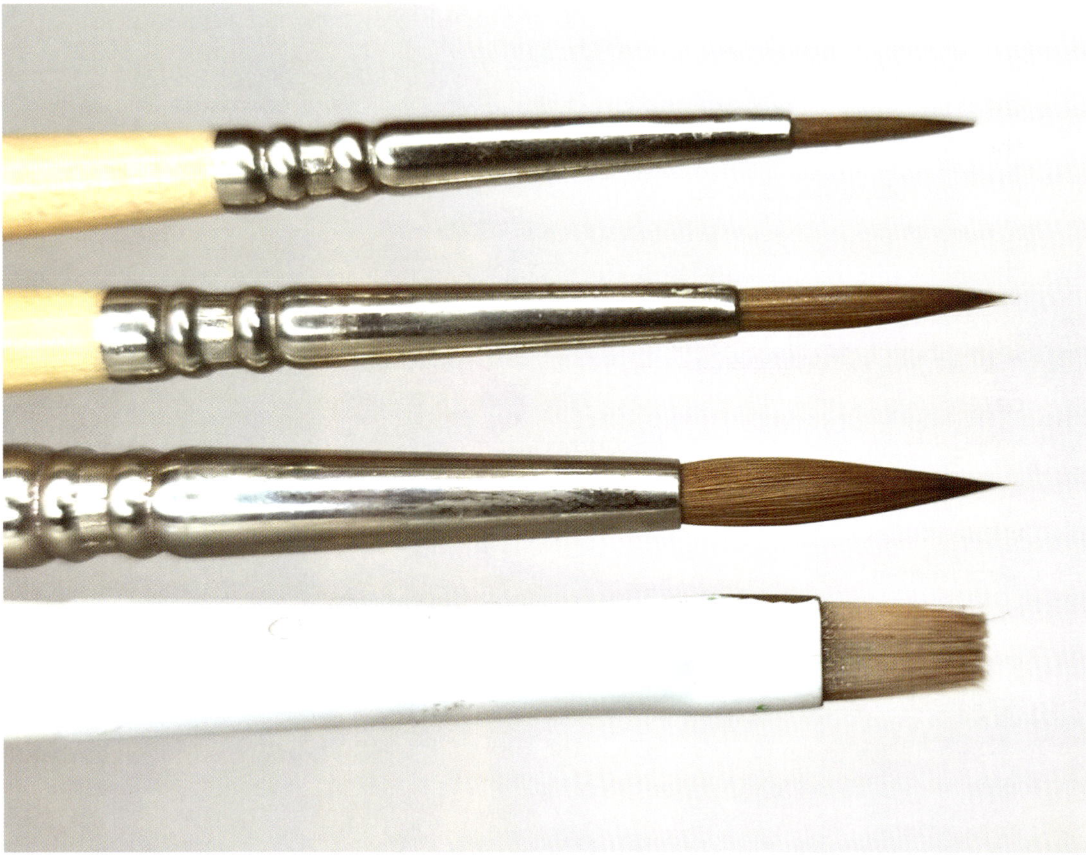

A high-quality brush will also give you better brush control and a finer finish. Personally, I mostly use the Winsor and Newton series 7, Rosemary and Co, and Broken Toad ranges. That said, for things like applying washes and drybrushing, I find simple, cheap hobby brushes from the craft shop to be perfectly adequate. For less expensive but still serviceable brushes, Pro Arte, Army Painter and Games Workshop all produce useful examples. It's worth having some cheap, disposable brushes too, for jobs like mixing paint, applying washes, drybrushing and applying glue – anything you do not want to use your best brushes for.

Paintbrushes themselves are typically made from either synthetic weave or natural hair. Synthetic brushes don't tend to hold paint as well as natural brushes, but when working with acrylic paint this isn't too much of a hindrance as you will be cleaning the brush anyway thanks to the rapid drying times of the medium. Natural brushes tend to give you better control over the application of paint and are better at retaining their point for precision application. They also hold more paint, giving the added benefit of being able to keep working on a subject for longer. Natural fibre bristles are at their best when used for detail work, especially painting areas such as faces or fine layered highlights.

As you work, you will naturally need to clean your brush. When using most acrylic paints a simple pot of water will be sufficient for use between changing colours and to prevent paint drying in the bristles. Regardless of what your brush's bristles are made from, I'd not recommend leaving it any longer than a few minutes between giving it a quick swish around in some water. You can add a little washing up liquid to your water too, although I've not found it necessary myself.

For more long-term care, there is a wide range of brush cleaners and conditioners on the market, and frequently there are products put out from each of the major paint ranges. It's worth investing in either some brush cleaner or better still, some brush soap to prevent excess wear or damage to your brushes' bristles. Odourless brush cleaner can be especially handy for helping to restore brushes. Each of these products will have its own set of specific instructions, usually printed on the side of the packaging, typically involving giving the brush a solid swishing around in the cleaner/soap, leaving it to stand for a bit and then rinsing clean and shaping. I've used a combination of brush soap with high-end sable brushes to keep them in use nearly every day for several years now!

With regard to what size and shape brush you should be getting, a size 0, a size 1 and a size 2 round should be sufficient. Although it may seem counterintuitive, a brush with a good quality point and fairly long bristles will be far more useful and give a much better result than a tiny size 000 for the vast majority of painting work.

You'll probably spot in the painting guides the use of flat brushes as well as make-up brushes and these are just what they sound like – either flat, chisel-like brushes or round, dense, short-haired brushes. They are both great for drybrushing as they give a good amount of control and lend themselves well to pulling over the raised detail, allowing you to have fairly precise highlights quickly. They aren't compulsory for drybrushing but do make life a lot easier.

PAINTING TECHNIQUES

Over the course of the painting guides, I'll be referring to several techniques. Rather than repeat myself in each guide, I'll cover a few of the basic ones here, and then they are ready for you to add to your toolbox.

DRYBRUSHING

Drybrushing is, as the name implies, the technique of using a small amount of paint on a dry brush to build up layers of colour by quickly flicking the brush over the surface of the model. This will have the effect of adding a contrasting colour to raised areas while leaving the remaining parts of the model in a darker tone.

Whilst simple in concept, it can take a little practice to become proficient with drybrushing. Although drybrushing implies a completely dry brush, this can lead to streaking or powdery paint. Having a slightly damp brush before loading it with paint can give a much smoother effect. It can be difficult to gauge just how much to moisten the brush, so the best thing to do is practise and find a level that works for you.

Once your paints are applied to the pallet, avoid thinning them and just load up the tip of the brush with a tiny amount of paint. Clean this paint from the brush with some tissues, then test to see how much paint is present by lightly dragging the bristles over some card. You want the paint to be landing on the tops of creases, folds and details of the model, but also want to avoid streaking or blobbing of paint. With drybrushing, it's best to allow several layers of paint to build up to achieve the effect you are aiming for as opposed to going in with one initial, heavy drybrush as this can overwhelm your model.

One tool I've found to be very useful for drybrushing is the make-up blusher brush as they have soft bristles and allow paint to build up into very nice gradients of colour.

WASHING AND GLAZING

A wash is a heavily thinned paint that flows and settles into the details of the model when applied. Washes can be purchased as ready mixed forms or you can make your own. To make a wash, simply add two to three parts of water with a little washing up liquid or flow improver to one part paint and then mix these together. Paint this mix over the model, letting it accumulate in recesses and details but not allowing it pool. Pooling can be caused by too much wash being applied and thus flooding the model.

A wash is best applied with an older though still well-shaped brush with soft bristles. If you apply too much wash, you can remove it by using a clean brush to soak up the excess paint before it dries.

A glaze or filter is a similar technique to a wash and is used to unify the highlights and shades already applied. The process is largely the same as applying a wash; however, it is applied far more sparingly. For applying a glaze, simply use a less heavily loaded brush than you would with a wash and paint this over the model, allowing the colour of the glaze to form on the model without flowing into the recesses as heavily as a wash.

This image demonstrates the difference between a model with a filter or glaze applied and one without. The darker vehicle at the top has had a glaze applied; otherwise, they are painted with the same techniques.

VARNISH

A varnish is a clear layer applied to the model to protect the paint finish during handling. Varnishes are essentially gloss, matt or satin in finish. Gloss is very shiny, matt is very flat and satin is somewhere in between and largely depends on the manufacturer as to where it falls between the two. Whether you use just one type of varnish, all three types or none at all is entirely up to you.

Varnishes can be obtained in many forms, but most useful for our purposes are those in spray cans. These allow you to varnish many models quickly and evenly, and also have the added bonus of generally being touch-dry reasonably quickly. Avoid spraying on hot or humid days, however, as this can cause the paint to cloud and potentially ruin your paint job!

Hopefully these tips and techniques will have you feeling confident about getting on with assembling and painting your models, and as ever, should be treated as a stepping-off point for your own experiments. Now on to actually building your models!

PAINTING GUIDES

Now that the basics of tools and preparation are covered, we can start to look at actually painting your models. For most of these guides I will mention the primer colour used, but these are not set in stone. If you have a primer you prefer using, or want to experiment with using coloured spray primers, then I encourage you to experiment as much as you can.

With such an extensive range of equipment in use during the war, and the varieties of paint scheme and quality of paint that were present, it would be impossible to cover every variation. However, each of the following guides will give you a good baseline for painting standard equipment for each nation covered in this book. Whilst this book is about painting armoured vehicles in general, the guides apply to soft-skins, artillery, logistical support and any other equipment that may have been used by the powers of the Second World War.

With so many scale models available that can work well with gaming, it seems useful to add a quick conversion table. Figure sizes aren't invariable;

one manufacturer's 28mm might be quite different to another's, and even more so when taking into account heft and build of individual figures, so their relation to ratio scales is always a little problematic. This is therefore a more-or-less guide rather than exact. Some sizes have a bit of a range in scales associated with them. It's fine to mix them, but best to remain consistent; for example, using all 1/56 or all 1/48 vehicles with your 28mm figures will look far better than a combination of the two. Also, the lower the number in the ratio, the larger the model: 1/285 means the subject is 285 times smaller than the real thing, whilst 1/56 means it is only 56 times smaller.

SCALE

Figure size	Ratio scale	Model railway scale
6mm	1/300–1/285	ZZ Gauge
10mm	1/160–1/144	N Gauge
15mm	1/100	TT Gauge, or HO Gauge
20mm	1/76–1/72	OO Guage
28mm	1/56–1/48	O Gauge
54mm	1/35–1/32	Gauge 1

2

British Vehicles

HISTORY

Whilst this book covers the period from 1943, I'll predominantly be focusing on the post-1944 paint schemes used by the British Army. This is because the locally applied patterns used in Italy and Tunisia are too varied for me to do justice to in this volume.

The paint schemes of British military vehicles were set out in a series of documents: Army Council Instructions (ACI) and Military Training Pamphlets (MTP). Through the course of the Second World War, the British Army went through a number of iterations of camouflage paint for their vehicles, which were both theatre and year dependent, as well as variations of pattern depending on the vehicle and regiment.

In Europe, during the initial phase of the war, these patterns started out as khaki with green stripes. From 1942 to 1944, this was gradually replaced by various patterns using brown and black. Document MTP.46 codified these schemes into an SCC 2 Brown and SCC 14 Black camouflage pattern. (SCC stands for Standard Camouflage Colour.) They were primarily intended to confound aerial observation, with the black paint used on upper and lower surfaces.

These camouflage patterns would remain on the vehicles until the end of 1944, predominantly seen on soft-skin and training vehicles. I've not come across any tanks camouflaged using MTP.46 patterns but there are a few photos that appear to have been taken in Normandy featuring armoured cars and Universal Carriers.

ACI.533, issued on 12 April 1944, heralded the introduction of the use of SCC 15. This tone was intended to match to the Olive Drab used on equipment supplied from the United States via Lend Lease. Although similar to the US Olive Drab colour, SCC 15 is considerably greener in tone, and does appear distinctly different.

SCC 15 was used on all equipment and was the standard paint used on British equipment from the Normandy campaign until the end of the war. Disruptive patterns were very rarely used, and applied at a unit level, if seen at all. If they were used, they are most likely to be seen painted onto soft-skin vehicles, armoured cars, and tank destroyers such as the Achilles.

One notable scheme, however, was the habit of applying a light grey or white disruptive pattern to roughly half the forward part of the 17-pdr gun used on the Sherman Fireflies. This was painted onto the lower part of the gun barrel in a wavy line, and intended to conceal the larger weapon these vehicles were equipped with, so that they would not stand out from the 75mm armed vehicles that made up the rest of their squadron.

As with the majority of armies, the British applied a temporary winter whitewash when weather conditions deemed this necessary.

The temporary nature of this paint meant that it could very quickly start to look ragged and worn.

Whilst the use of disruptive pattern camouflage paint was rare with the British Army in Northern Europe, the use of netting and foliage was not. British armour can often be seen with heavy use of camouflage netting with hessian strips woven through it. This is usually applied to the turret, but can also be seen on the vehicles' hulls.

As a force primarily involved with offensive operations, British vehicles are often seen loaded with stowage. One distinctive pattern of stowage that seems to separate them from American equipment is the frequent application of additional track links as extra armour, especially amongst Sherman and Churchill tanks. This makeshift protection is typically affixed to turret sides and hull fronts, and can even be seen to be making use of captured German track link.

INSIGNIA AND TACTICAL MARKINGS

The British Army used an extensive system of insignia and tactical marks on their vehicles. Broadly speaking, you would have the Allied star on the upper surface – the turret or cab roof being the most common placements. For armoured vehicles, there would be a geometric squadron marking applied to either the turret or hull side, and were shape and colour-coded for both regiment and squadron. Further along the sides, though, also sometimes on the front of the vehicle, would be the serial number. This would be a corresponding letter followed by a series of identifying numbers. A tank, for example, would have T, then a series of digits. These were usually painted in letters about 3 inches high, though that would of course vary depending on how much space there was on the actual vehicle.

On the front and rear would often be seen a regimental or divisional badge, such as the famous Desert Rat of the 7th Armoured Division. Alongside this would be the regimental badge, typically a square, colour-coded to the brigade type, and then a number painted within this showing which regiment they belonged to. Within an armoured brigade, for example, this took the form of a red square, with the number being either 51, 52 or 53, depending on the regiment's seniority. HQ vehicles would have the number 50.

Finally, a yellow disc with the vehicle's weight class was also applied to the front. Note, these do not specify the actual weight of the vehicle but correspond to a system of classification for use with bridging and shipping systems.

It's worth noting that some, none or all of these symbols could be used on a vehicle. Each division had its own particular system of presenting this information within these frameworks, so positioning and application could vary widely. Additionally, extra markings could also be applied, such as turret roofs being painted white during Operation Goodwood, or 27th Armoured Brigade utilising double-digit red-and-white numbers on their Shermans' turrets during the Normandy campaign. I'd recommend spending a little time refining your research if you want to model a particular unit during a particular campaign as the variations are pretty wide.

Here are two painting guides to applying an SCC 15 scheme to a vehicle. The first is designed for brush application and the second is for airbrush use. This guide is intended to give you a clean-looking vehicle. You can add any of the weathering techniques and options covered later in this book to the finished model, depending on your personal taste.

BRUSH METHOD

1 Prime black

Firstly, begin by spraying the model with some black primer. You could alternatively use an Olive Drab spray and skip the next step; however, I prefer working from black. This brings a more interesting and rich colour to the model, and adds some more depth to the shadows and details. If you want to get the models on the table quicker, though, use

the Olive Drab or SCC 15 spray. Tamiya do a good range of aerosol cans that are good colour matches for Second World War models.

Brush used	Paint
Aerosol can	Citadel Chaos Black or Tamiya TS-28 Olive Drab

2 Drybrush base

We will now use a large stippling brush (make-up brushes are ideal for this) to apply the SCC 15 colour using a stippling action. Work in layers, from the centre of the panels outwards. The idea here isn't so much to pick up detail but to get a base of colour down with the deepest recesses remaining in black. The beauty of using this particular method is that it will lay the foundation for some texture to the paint and give the effect of cast or rolled steel.

Brush used	Paint
Large make-up brush	AK 11386 SCC 15 Olive Drab

3 Intermediate tone

If you wish to skip this step, you can go straight to Step 4. To add an extra level of volume to the SCC 15, using a medium-sized, soft make-up brush you can stipple on a lighter mid-olive colour. Apply this with the same stippling technique used in Step 2, allowing the olive base tone to show through. The intent is to add a more interesting and varied surface to the model.

Brush used	Paint
Medium make-up brush	AK 11309 Olivgrün

4 Edge light

Using a medium-sized flat brush, apply a light drybrush to emphasise the detail. Using a pale green-grey colour, lightly drybrush the model, concentrating the drybrushing along the edges of the armour plates and the raised details. Be careful not to have the paint streaking or blotching in the centre of the armour plates. With this step complete, you can

move on to adding the panel line detail to the model, using either oils or acrylics, detailed later in this chapter.

Brush used	Paint
Large flat brush	Vallejo 886 Green Grey

5 Olive green wash

If you wish, you can now tone down the contrast between colours with a thin layer of the original SCC 15 colour, applied as a glaze or thin wash. This will serve to level out all the previous steps. When applying, you can put the paint on fairly heavily and then lift it off with your brush when it starts to pool.

Brush used	Paint
Size 4 round	AK 11386 SCC 15 Olive Drab

AIRBRUSH

For the airbrush method, I'll use the same paints as with the brush method. Whilst lacquer-based paints such as those produced by Tamiya, Mr Hobby and AK Interactive are very good, they aren't particularly beginner friendly as they require specialised thinners and cleaner.

1 Spray black

Again, apply a black primer to the model. You can either airbrush or use a rattle can to apply this. I tend to use rattle cans for gaming models as they provide a harder-wearing base layer to work from.

Brush used	Paint
Aerosol can	Citadel Chaos Black

2 Apply SCC 15 Olive Drab

To start, airbrush on a light coat of the olive colour. This will be much darker than the actual final tone but it will give a good key for subsequent layers.

Once this initial pass of colour has dried, spray the Olive Drab to pick out the details, working in light passes, allowing the colour to increase in opacity, with the strongest tone in the centre of armour panels.

Brush used	Paint
Sparmax Max-4	AK 11386 SCC 15 Olive Drab

3 First level of highlight

Using the lighter olive colour, we will now apply a light olive green coat into the centre of armour panels, areas of details, hatches and so on. If you wish to start adding a more weathered effect to the finish, apply the paint in a more mottled style on the flat surfaces and in streaky vertical lines along the sides.

Brush used	Paint
Sparmax Max-4	AK 11309 Olivgrün

4 Final highlight

To really enhance the details, and colour volumes of the model, apply a final highlight. Spray this into the previously highlighted areas. Allow the paint to build up in the most prominent areas, and also anywhere that would naturally catch the light. You can also use this to enhance the mottling and streaking applied in the previous stage.

Brush used	Paint
Sparmax Max-4	Vallejo 886 Green Grey

5 Filter layer

If the model has too much contrast between the tones, or you feel the paint has moved too far from the original SCC 15 colour, you can apply a filter tone of the base colour.

To make a filter out of conventional paint you will need to thin it much more heavily than usual. When airbrushing the paint on, lightly mist it on in layers. You do not want to spray too heavily as it will flood the model. Apply a layer, let it settle, and then apply another layer, letting the tone build up until you are happy with the model's appearance.

Brush used	Paint
Sparmax Max-4	AK 11386 SCC 15 Olive Drab

TOOLS

Whilst the tools would typically be painted the same colour as the rest of the vehicle, the model will look better if they are picked out in a separate colour. I prefer to use a lighter tone so that they stand out more. For

metal tools, I prefer to pick them out with a lighter version of the main colour of the vehicle; for any wooden parts, such as spade hafts, I pick out with a wood tone.

For extra detail, you can add some chipping by painting along the edges of the tools with a dark metal tone. I prefer to use either a gunmetal grey or a metallic black.

Brush used	Paint
Size 1 round	Vallejo 924 Russian Uniform (metal tools)
Size 1 round	Vallejo 976 Buff
Size 1 round	Vallejo 073 Metallic Black

PINWASHING

Before adding the pinwashing, it is worth applying decals to the model. This will help them blend into the model and prevent them looking like stickers on a toy.

To enhance the details on the vehicle further, you can apply a wash to them. There are many ways to do this and I'll cover a few methods through the course of this book. You can use any of the wash methods for any of the nationalities. It's entirely down to personal choice. I'll demonstrate both acrylic and oil paint methods for these particular vehicles. You can use either of these methods, whether you have drybrushed or airbrushed the model.

Acrylic wash

Acrylics can be difficult to use for pinwashing, although they are quick, clean and non-toxic as well as requiring less specialised cleaning supplies.

When applying an acrylic pinwash, you'll have to work very quickly, and ideally have two brushes ready. Using a premixed wash makes things much simpler here. Apply the wash into panel lines and around details, working in small areas. How small an area will be down to the paint you're using and how quickly you can work. While the wash is still wet, using a damp brush blend out the edges so that it does not create tidemarks. Alternatively, you can paint the wash over all or a small part of the model and then lift it from the model before it dries. Again, you will need to be quick with how you work here, and work on small sections at a time.

A dark brown tone will work best for most Second World War vehicles.

Brush used	Paint
Size 2 round	Games Workshop Agrax Earthshade

Oil wash

Artists' oils are much more forgiving to work with when applying pinwashes. They have very long drying times and can be reactivated days later using white spirit. Oils can be more aggressive, so it's worth ensuring your model is fully dried before applying them. This is especially true with airbrushed paints, which result in a much thinner layer of paint so need a few days to harden fully before you do anything further with them.

After mixing the oil wash, apply it into and around the details. You will find that capillary action really assists the paint in flowing into where you

want it to go. Once the wash has become touch-dry, usually after an hour or two, you can then use a brush lightly dampened in thinners to remove any excess paint. You can then leave the model overnight, or ideally, for a day or two, and then go on to do any further weathering you may wish to add.

Again, use a dark brown to mix the wash.

Brush used	Paint
Size 1 round	Windsor & Newton Burnt Umber

Canadian Universal Carrier; note the upside-down star. This was sometimes applied to Canadian vehicles as a national marking.

British Universal Carrier. This vehicle has a hand-painted disruptive camouflage pattern in black.

Churchill Mk.VI troop. These vehicles are each painted slightly differently but maintain a unified appearance through having the same weathering and stowage.

A34 Comet.

Cromwell.

Dingo Scout Car.

Sherman Firefly Vc.

Canadian 6pdr and Loyd Carrier.

M5 half-track.

M4A4 Sherman V.

3

United States Vehicles

HISTORY

The United States Army had been using one variation or another of Olive Drab from prior to the First World War. Whilst often portrayed as a very dark green, especially in older colour plates, this is largely the result of incorrect interpretation of colour. The General Headquarters of the Army officially ratified Olive Drab in 1918. This tone was created from the black and ochre pigments, and described as 'the colour of pig slop' (Zaloga, *Military Modelling*, 2002). Through the interwar period, the paint became a gloss version of Olive Drab, as this was harder wearing and looked smarter. However, with tensions rising across the world in the late 1930s and early 40s, a new paint finish was sought.

This new chemical formulation was essentially the same tone as the pre-war colour, although due to the gloss nature of the previous paint, the new version appeared somewhat lighter. This new paint, Olive Drab No.9 as it was known from 1942, was a dark olive colour, which is distinctly browner than it is green in appearance. It also faded and weathered, giving a somewhat varied appearance in final colour on the vehicle.

Olive Drab No.9 didn't have much in the way of terms of official variation through the war and was used universally on all manner of equipment. Artillery, tanks, trucks, ammunition boxes, jerry cans, helmets and even grenades were all finished in Olive Drab No.9. That said, towards the end of 1944, a slightly darker version appeared that became more common on the later vehicles, such as the M26 Pershing, M4A3E8 Sherman and M18 Hellcat.

Disruptive patterns of camouflage were both authorised and recommended, though not universal. Many, if not even most, vehicles were finished in the standard Olive Drab paint. Field Manual *FM 5-20B: Camouflage of Vehicles* provided detailed instructions on how to camouflage vehicles, giving different templates for various combat vehicles, notably Shermans, M10 Tank Destroyers and M7 Priests. As with any camouflage pattern, these were intended to break up the outline of the vehicle, and achieved this with large, sweeping shapes in a contrasting colour. In North Africa and Italy, these patterns utilised various brown and tan tones, but in Northwestern Europe, this pretty much exclusively featured a black overspray on top of the Olive Drab. First utilised with the 2nd Armoured Division during Operation Cobra in July 1944, these patterns would appear on combat vehicles until the end of the war. Interestingly, they do not appear on soft-skin vehicles, and are unusual to see on lighter armour as well.

During the harsh winter of 1944, the US Army used winter whitewash. This was a water-soluble paint, applied by troops in the field. *FM 5-20B* gives camouflage patterns for use with winter whitewash and suggests using a similar disruptive pattern to that of the other camouflage schemes, with broad swathes of white applied over the base paint. In practice, however, troops seem to have applied rough coats of white, using whatever tools they had to hand to apply the paint. Few units seem to have used the disruptive scheme, most likely due to time constraints. This whitewash would frequently overpaint tactical and unit markings on the subject vehicle too.

American vehicles would make use of netting and foliage for camouflage; although not that common with them during combat action, you do see it more often on the tank destroyers. Crews often fitted additional protection to their vehicles, especially to Shermans. Although not recommended, or even authorised in some cases, due to the additional weight and strain it would place on a vehicle's drive train, this improvised protection does appear throughout the 1944–5 period. Some protective upgrades actually became quite extensive. Sandbags were common, to the extent of a wall of sandbags along all vertical surfaces apart from the rear, held in place by a welded-on series of frames. I've seen this applied to both 75mm and 76mm armed Shermans, as well as Easy 8s. Other methods of improvised protection include a thick layer of concrete applied to the front of a tank's hull, spare track links or salvaged armour welded to the front of the vehicle, or logs fitted to the sides of the turret and hull. How much protection these systems may have provided is open to debate, but were probably helpful to the crew's morale at least.

Stowage is frequently seen on and associated with American vehicles – perhaps more so than with any other nation's equipment. It can really help to reinforce that a vehicle is in American service to have it loaded up with equipment. In general terms, this equipment would be stored on the engine deck, front of the hull, turret sides and rear of the hull, on a small stowage shelf. Stowage was rarely hung from the sides of the hull as it could be easily damaged or lost while traversing terrain.

For markings, the Americans used a series of five pointed stars, as well as a series of letters and symbols to denote to which unit the vehicle belonged. Serial numbers were also applied to vehicles, and it was relatively common for crews to name their vehicle, too – at least for tank crews. Nominally, armoured vehicles were to have one star on either side of the hull and turret, one on the front of the hull, and one on the turret roof or engine deck. These could then be surrounded by either a complete or segmented circle, again in white. In Normandy, there was a concern that the Germans may have used gas weaponry, so some vehicles, especially jeeps and half-tracks, had their fill around the edge of the star and outlining circle on the engine hoods painted an ochre yellow. This paint was intended to change colour in the presence of poison gas. Given how conspicuous these markings were, however, some or all (except those used for air recognition) would be either omitted or concealed in some way. This concealment could take the form of covering the national markings with mud or grease, painting them black, or using camouflage netting or stowage to obscure them.

With regard to painting these two Shermans, I'll add camouflage to both to illustrate methods of how to apply it with or without an airbrush. For these vehicles, we will be using a slightly used and faded version of Olive Drab.

BRUSH METHOD

1 Prime the model

To begin with, you will require an initial layer of paint on the model. As with the other guides, I prefer to use black, although you could use an Olive Drab spray instead. I find the black gives a better base to work from, especially for painting hard-to-reach areas such as tracks and suspension.

Brush used	Paint
Aerosol can	Citadel Chaos Black or Tamiya TS-28 Olive Drab

2 Olive Drab base

Using a broad, soft brush, start building up layers of Olive Drab. You will probably need to thin your paint. The amount of added water required will depend on the paint you are using, but you will want a consistency that flows smoothly from the brush. When applying the paint, this may require two or three layers to get a fully opaque tone. Try to be neat and avoid any pooling or flooding of details. If you've sprayed the model with Olive Drab instead, you can skip this stage.

Brush used	Paint
Size 4 round	AK 11339 Olive Drab

3 Mid-tone

We will now use a medium-sized make-up brush to stipple on a medium green/grey colour. This will be quite high contrast with the Olive Drab, but this is intentional. Ensure that you aren't causing the paint to streak

as you apply it, and built it up in layers, allowing the details to become prominent and contrasted with the base paints.

Brush used	Paint
Medium make-up brush	Vallejo 886 Green Grey

4 Edge light

Using a light greenish grey, now use the same make-up brush to apply some edge highlights to the model. As this Sherman is an M4A1 with cast hull, there are fewer hard edges to pick up with a drybrush, but we can still use the technique to enhance the details.

Brush used	Paint
Medium make-up brush	Vallejo 885 Pastel Green

5 Olive green filter

This will now be looking fairly pale, and you may wish to keep the model like this to represent a well-worn and faded vehicle, but if you wish to

unify the tones and bring things back a bit, we can apply a filter. A filter is a thin layer of paint, applied evenly over a model, as opposed to a wash, where the intention is to enhance the recesses. This will bring about a levelling and unifying of the colours instead.

Brush used	Paint
Size 4 round	AK 11339 Olive Drab

6 Black camouflage

If you wish to apply camouflage to the vehicle, you can do so now. Whilst you could use conventional black paint, I like to use one of the new generation of contrast or speed paints that are currently available, as this will allow some of the shading and highlight already applied to show through. I've used Citadel Black Legion, which is a very matt, opaque black. However there are similar black paints from various manufacturers that could be used.

Apply the paint evenly, and in fairly broad, sweeping shapes that contrast with the shapes and angles of the vehicle. Some of these types of paint may not be as hardwearing, so you could apply a clear coat of varnish at this stage if you wish. You could also use this paint to pick out the tools, machine guns, and tracks.

Brush used	Paint
Size 4 round	Citadel Black Legion

AIRBRUSH METHOD

1 Spray black

Whilst we could use a primer from a spray can, this time we will airbrush on the primer layer, again using black. Ensure you are wearing a respirator and have a well-ventilated area when applying primers with an airbrush, as they can contain some nasty chemicals. Ensure you cover the figure evenly and that you have a smooth black layer as a base to work on.

Brush used	Paint
Sparmax Max-4	Vallejo 602 Black Primer

2 Olive Drab base

We will now spray the tank with Olive Drab. Work along armour panels and plates, letting the tone increase whilst leaving the shaded areas dark, or even black. A good way to do this is by spraying a light coat of Olive

Drab over the entire model and then working on ever-increasing small areas to enhance the details and levels of shadow.

Brush used	Paint
Sparmax Max-4	AK 11339 Olive Drab

3 Apply mid-tone

If you wanted the Sherman to look like a freshly issued vehicle, then you could stop at this stage and proceed to adding some panel lining to detail it. However, we will now start to apply some subtle fading and weathering to the paint finish on the model. Using a green-grey paint, we will apply some lighter areas to the sides of the vehicle, as well as anywhere that is going to catch the light on the flat surfaces (turret and hull roofs, hatches etc.). When working at the sides, apply the paint in vertical lines and create a mottled, streaky effect to the tank's surface.

Brush used	Paint
Sparmax Max-4	Vallejo 886 Green Grey

4 Light tone

Again, you could call the model finished, prior to applying this stage. If you want to replicate a slightly faded vehicle, or a later war vehicle in the slightly darker, very late war tone, you can ignore this stage and go on to the filter stage.

To really enhance the highlights we added in the previous step, you can apply some limited and very focused highlights to the tank. Apply

the paint to the most prominent areas that catch the light the most. You can also add this to some of the streaks and mottling applied to the side, although apply this sparingly as you do not want the tank to appear too pale.

Brush used	Paint
Sparmax Max-4	Vallejo 885 Pastel Green

5 Camouflage

To apply the black disruptive pattern you can either freehand the black onto the model or mask the scheme before you spray it. Whilst you could use tape or blue/white tack, these can have a tendency to damage the paint below. Tamiya/Kabuki tape is ideal for modelling use. However, artist's tape can be a little too sticky, so it may be worth de-tacking it before applying. There are very good modelling putties designed for masking available, too. Panzer Putty from AK Interactive is very good.

For this model, though, I've applied the camouflage by eye, as I like a rougher edge to the disruptive patterns.

Brush used	Paint
Sparmax Max-4	AK 11029 Black

TOOLS

These are very similar in process to the tools on the British vehicles, and everything said in that chapter applies here as well. Essentially, pick out the tools, gun barrels, tracks and tyres of the wheels in black, and then pick out the details with their relevant colours.

I like to paint them with a mid-tone of paint and then use the oil and weathering stages to tie them into the rest of the vehicle.

Brush used	Paint
Size 1 round	Vallejo 924 Russian Uniform (metal tools)
Size 1 round	Vallejo 976 Buff
Size 1 round	Vallejo 073 Metallic Black

PINWASHING

Acrylic method

In the British vehicle guide, we used a brown wash to apply the pinwashing to the vehicle, and on this tank, we will use black. This will add a deeper level of contrast, but where the model has black as part of its disruptive pattern, it is worth having that extra level of contrast as it can help to unify how the model looks. Again, work in small, limited areas, and blend the wash out before it can dry. Capillary action will also help you to get the paint flowing where you want it to be.

Brush used	Paint
Size 2 round	Citadel Nuln Oil

Oil method

With the British guide, we used Burnt Umber to apply a neat wash to the model. This time, we will apply an all-over wash and then use an old brush to clean up the model. This will result in a more weathered appearance to the tank. If you are going to use this method, it's worth applying the transfers to the model first. It's also worth giving the model a clear coat of varnish before applying this method as it can be quite hard on acrylic paints.

1 Oil wash

After mixing the wash as detailed in the British pinwash section, apply this using an older brush evenly over the entire model. Ensure you get the wash into all the details and recesses.

Brush used	Paint
Old size 4 round	Windsor & Newton Burnt Umber

2 Cleaning up

Leave the model to become touch-dry; this should take a few hours. You can leave it overnight and then come back to it the following morning if you wish, as oils are easy to reactivate. To remove the paint, get a small amount of thinner and dampen your brush. Move the brush over the surface of the model to remove paint from areas where you do not want it. You are essentially aiming to mop up the paint as well as to create smooth transitions from areas of shadow and recesses.

On this model, I've used vertical motions to help enhance the streaking on the sides of the turret and hull of the tank. This is also a good way to start your weathering process if you want a grimy looking vehicle.

Brush used	Product
Old size 4 round	White spirit

M4A1 Shermans. These are painted to represent the majority of Shermans used during the Second World War.

M26 Pershing.

M10 Tank Destroyer Platoon.

M4A1 76mm, summer 1944.

M4A1 Sherman, summer 1944.

Willys Jeep. These vehicles are configured for a reconnaissance role.

M5 Stuart.

4

Russian Vehicles

HISTORY

Whilst Russian vehicles may appear amongst the simplest to paint and are generally regarded as being an olive green tone with the occasional patriot slogan on the turret or superstructure, the reality is somewhat more complex. For such a ubiquitous paint colour, utilised by one of the major powers of the Second World War, 4BO Green, the paint used by the Russians, has proven remarkably difficult to pin down to a specific tone. There is a lot of contradictory and vague information regarding this colour, and a definitive answer has eluded experts for decades. This is due to a variety of reasons; access to Soviet records has been a significant problem and paint chips of surviving vehicles are prone to ageing and weathering, so display a variety of tones. These factors, combined with personal photography, especially colour photography, being far less prevalent in the Soviet Union, have made research difficult.

Fortunately, there are a few consistencies we can draw upon. Importantly, we have the official paint mix for making 4BO Green. The pigments used are yellow ochre, zinc chromate, white and ultramarine. Mixed together in various ratios, these all result in a relatively light olive green tone. Where things get complicated is that most paint samples are a much darker olive tone. It has been suggested that this is due to a chemical reaction, with the 4BO paint appearing to darken with age. Surviving paint chips are a relatively dark olive green that ranges from blue to browner tones but are all roughly in a similar tonal range. In terms of appearance, these tend to be a little lighter than the Olive Drabs used by Britain and the United States, and also either bluer, or yellower, depending on the particular colour chip being referenced.

4BO paint was used as a primer as well as the primary paint on Russian equipment and could be found on pretty much all vehicles, helmets, ammunition boxes and so on. The finish has been described as both smooth and very hardwearing. It was developed in about 1939 and was intended to be used as part of a camouflage scheme utilising 6K Dark Brown and 7K Green Black. However, few vehicles were finished in this scheme, though it was more prevalent on artillery pieces.

A new camouflage pattern was introduced in 1941, although due to logistical disruption, it seems it was not used until 1943–4. This new scheme again used the 4BO Green as a base, with 7K Yellow (a sandy or earth yellow tone) and 6K Dark Brown used as disruptive colours. Approximately 50 per cent of equipment retained the green, with the rest of the surface broken up with spots or broad swatches of disruptive colours. There was no uniformity to these patterns and the intent was that design decisions would be made at local level, and appropriate to the equipment being painted in a way that would break up angles and shapes to make observation more difficult. Due to shortages, sometimes patterns would emerge that utilised either the 7K Yellow or 6K Dark Brown in a two-tone scheme applied over the green.

Evidence for these schemes can be hard to find, although they do appear in the southern sector of the Eastern Front fighting in the summer of 1944 as well as in other theatres of war. I suspect that due to the similarity of tone of these colours, especially the dark brown, they may be hard to pick out in black-and-white photographs of the era, especially if a vehicle has a layer of dust on it. However, assault guns and artillery pieces do seem to have been the more common recipients of camouflage paint, whilst logistical support units do not. Tanks can sometimes be seen with this patterning, although it is quite hard to spot and when it does appear, is most common on light and medium tanks such as the T-34.

It's worth noting that post war, the Russians changed their green paint again and introduced another subtle difference, this time being a much browner, more olive colour, which whilst similar to the colour used in the Second World War, is also quite different.

Modellers and wargamers have something of a tendency to assume Russian vehicles were substantially heavily weathered and prone to severe rusting and wear. This is an artistic choice and doesn't have much connection to the historical evidence, with Russian vehicles being as clean or as worn as any other belligerent's equipment. This most likely stems from the images of Russian vehicle storage parks from the post-Soviet era in various states of disrepair. Lend Lease vehicles supplied from Britain and the United States generally retained their original paint and were not repainted with Russian versions of essentially the same colour.

In terms of insignia, Russian equipment had a few different commonly seen patterns of tactical markings and badges. Interestingly, the red star was rarely used as an identifier, especially post 1941. Occasionally, however, it can be seen painted onto vehicles as a white star, though in a smaller and slightly different pattern to that seen on Allied equipment in Western Europe.

Patriotic slogans appear often, as do tactical numbers. These slogans were typically hand painted, and featured some motivational or inspiring phrase, although they could also be statements of who had paid for or manufactured the particular machine. Numbers normally appear to take one of two forms: either small tactical signs within a geometrical shape such as a diamond, or larger, two, three or four-digit serials painted on the turret or casemate of the machine. These would denote the individual unit's place within its overall formation. They were depicted in white paint during the summer and could be repainted with red once the winter camouflage was applied.

Unit badges were also applied. These could be small geometric shapes or pictures of animals, painted as either solid forms or white outlines. Guards units can sometimes be identified by their use of formation-specific signs. These would vary from unit to unit, and could consist of a red star with bear, or crested red star with a banner behind it, or even simple geometric shapes, depending on the particular unit.

In the closing stages of the war, with Russian and Allied air supremacy dominating the battlefield, white identification marks were applied to the turrets or casemates of assault guns. These took the form of a white line at roughly midway up the side of the turret, or casemate in the case of self-propelled guns, and then could be either circles, triangles or some combination thereof painted on the roof of the turret. These were most commonly seen in the Berlin campaign.

White camouflage was ubiquitous in the harsh winters of the Eastern Front, and as with other nations, was employed as a temporary paint. Most of the time, this temporary camouflage was applied all over the vehicle. However, there are examples of more interesting patterns – either large white swatches showing the green underneath or more complex patterns created by the crews. The Russians made extensive use of natural camouflage, often using cut-down trees and bushes, although they do not appear to have used camouflage netting much on their vehicles.

For this model, I'll be using a green tone that I feel is pretty reflective of a generic 4BO Green, but I've also added examples of models painted with other variants of the colour, as well as some camouflaged vehicles. The camouflage pattern application will be the same as those in the German and American sections of this book.

NO AIRBRUSH METHOD

1 Spray Olive Drab or black

We will start by spraying the T-34. There are Russian green sprays, or you could use black. A dark olive base will give you a nice tone to work up from, as well as making a speedier job of painting the model. However, black will give you a richer colour and deeper recesses, especially when using a stippling method to get the next colours onto the model. Therefore, I have primed this T-34 in black.

Brush used	Paint
Aerosol can	Citadel Chaos Black or Tamiya TS-28 Olive Drab

2 Stipple on 4BO

To get our tank much closer to the proper colour, now stipple on some 4BO Green. There are many commercially available types of 4BO, and they are all a bit different. I like this one from the AK 3rd Gen line, but have a look through some photos and references and see which one looks closest to your eye.

Brush used	Paint
Size 4 round, make-up brush	AK 11368 Russian Green 4BO

3 Drybrush middle highlight

This is an optional step but can give you a more graduated highlight effect. We will be mixing some paint using a roughly 50:50 ratio of olive and a lighter green. This will give some more depth to the model's finish and help to reduce the contrast between the tones of this step and the next.

Brush used	Paint
Size 4 round, make-up brush	AK Gen 11368 Russian Green 4BO mixed with Vallejo 882 Middlestone

4 Edge highlight

NowI use the lighter green used in the mix in Step 3. This will be a very focused drybrush concentred around the edges and details and is intended to enhance those features without interfering with the base colours already applied. This is the time to apply any transfers and move on to adding any detail painting you may wish to add.

Brush used	Paint
Size 3 flat	Vallejo 882 Middlestone

5 Olive green filter

You can now apply a filter to smooth out the previously drybrushed colours. Here I've used a darker olive green to create a deeper version of 4BO. The airbrush method will demonstrate the lighter version of 4BO green. Simply mix the paint with some thinner or water and apply it in an even layer over the tank.

Brush used	Paint
Size 3 round	AK 1139 Olive Drab

AIRBRUSH METHOD

For this tank, we will be creating a slightly different shade of 4BO. This one will be a little lighter and yellower than the other.

1 Spray black

To make life a little easier in the next step, we can work from a black base. The green will be built up in several thin layers of spray, so it will be much easier to do this from black rather than green as this time we want more depth to the colour. I've used an aerosol primer for speed and efficiency, although you can of course airbrush on the primer instead if you wish.

Brush used	Paint
Aerosol can	Citadel Chaos Black or airbrush black primer

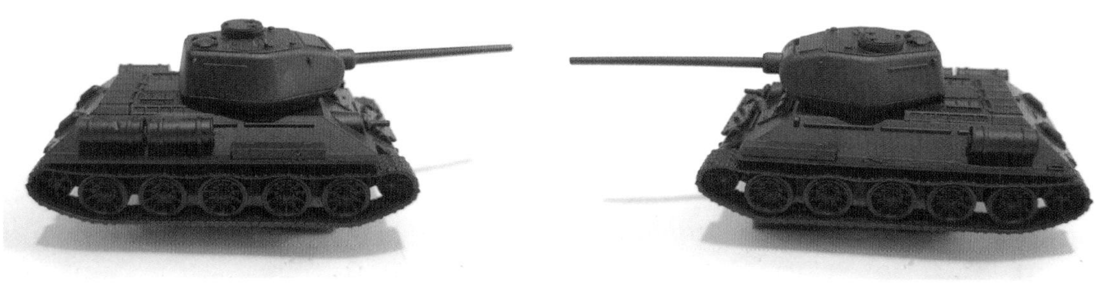

2 Spray base

The next stage is to airbrush on the 4BO Green. Keep the layers thin. Start by applying an overall pass with the airbrush of the green and letting it dry for a few minutes. This will give your additional layers something for them to key into. Then start to build up opacity by spraying the paint along the panel lines and around details. If you want a more weathered look to the model, you can leave the edges of the armour plates a little darker, as these can be enhanced with weathering later on.

Brush used	Paint
Sparmax Max-4	AK 11368 Russian Green 4BO

3 Spray mid-tone

We will now mix a highlight colour into our base. I'm going to use a greenish ochre tone, though you could use a lighter greyish or bluish green instead. However, to me this looks a good mix for 4BO. I've done an approximately 50:50 mix and then thinned the paint to a smooth consistency. It's hard to give specifics on thinning as there are so many variables with airbrushing. The best advice is to spray a test and see how well it's working.

Brush used	Paint
Sparmax Max-4	AK 11368 Russian Green 4BO and Vallejo 882 Middlestone

4 Apply streaking and enhance details

To add further depth to the green and some more contrast, we can apply a layer of the lighter colour used in the previous step. You do not need to do this stage, but I recommend it, especially when applying weathering as it will remove some of the contrast between tones. Airbrush the lightest tone around edges of panels and details, and add some vertical streaking if you want a more weathered or worn-looking finish. Now is the time to apply the some turret number transfers.

Brush used	Paint
Sparmax Max-4	Vallejo 882 Middlestone

5 Filter

Finally, we can unify all the colours with a glaze or filter of the base tone. In this case, I've used 4BO, but you could use Olive Drab if you want to create a darker version of 4BO Green.

Brush used	Paint
Sparmax Max-4	AK 11368 Russian Green 4BO

WHITE TACTICAL MARKINGS

Freehand method

These markings were crudely applied to the vehicle so there are a few methods to apply them. The first is simply to paint them on using some white paint. Paint a rough line around the middle of the turret and then an appropriate tactical marking on the turret roof. Keep the paint thin so that you have control, and apply it neatly. You can always come back and add more layers to improve the opacity of the colour. If you want to enhance the crudeness of the paint job, you can even add a few paint streaks if you wish.

Brush used	Paint
Size 2 round	AK 11001 White

Masked method

If you aren't confident in applying the markings freehand, you can use masking tape to mask out the areas you want to be white, and then either airbrush or stipple the paint on. This can be a little more time consuming, but gives a good effect. It's definitely worth adding a clear coat, though, if you've added transfers, as there's a danger the masking tape could damage them. It's probably worth de-tacking the tape on a piece of card or plastic before applying it over any transfers, just to be sure. Once you remove the tape, you can also add vertical lines to make it appear as if the paint has run. I have also stippled a little paint around the edges to make them appear more ragged.

Brush used	Paint
Size 2 round, small round make-up brush, or airbrush	AK 11001 White

DETAILING WASHES

Oil Paint Method

1 Apply wash

You can use several different types of wash, as detailed in the other parts of this book. For Russian vehicles, I'd recommend tones that lean towards grey and brown for pinwashing or surface washes. With oil paints, I strongly recommend a colour such as Payne's Grey. This will have the effect of darkening the colours a little, without actually changing the tone of the paint to another shade.

Here, I've painted the model with a layer of Payne's Grey, and after leaving it to dry for a few hours, I will remove most of the paint with a cotton bud lightly soaked in thinner.

Brush used	Paint
Size 4 round	Windsor & Newton Payne's Grey

2 Remove oil wash

Now, you can remove the touch-dry oil paint with a cotton bud. You will probably require several cotton buds, as once each one is full of paint you will need to swap it for a clean one. Lightly soak the bud in white spirit, then use it to polish off the oil paint until you have a level of patina that you like.

CLAY WASH

Whilst you can use oils to apply pinwashes, or acrylics if you wish, increasingly available are clay-based washes. These perform somewhere between oils and acrylics in that they are highly pigmented but dry comparatively quickly. Once applied, they become touch-dry in about twenty minutes and stay workable for a few hours, though how long depends on the particular brand.

1 Apply wash

Here, I've applied the wash fairly heavily onto the model, letting it flood around details and into panel lines. Once the wash has dried, and has a matt appearance, you can use a cotton bud dampened in water to buff off the excess wash.

Brush used	Paint
Size 2 round	Ultimate Weathering Products Dark Dirt

2 Removal of wash

As with the oil paint method, we will now remove the wash. I've left the model for about thirty to forty minutes, until it appears touch-dry. Unlike with oils, I've lightly dampened the cotton bud in water, although I am still using it to buff the surface free of the clay, replacing the cotton bud as necessary.

T-34/76 in two-tone camouflage. This vehicle also has the crest of a Guards Armoured formation on its turret.

KV-1 Heavy Tank.

KV-2 Heavy Tank.

T-34/76.

T-70 Light Tank. This vehicle uses the three-tone camouflage, and can be replicated using the methods detailed in the German chapter.

T-34/85. This vehicle has the recognition markings used in the advance on Berlin.

T-34/76 Model 1941.

5

German Vehicles

HISTORY

Typically, when German armour from the Second World War is presented in popular media, especially older media, it is painted in Panzer Grey (or Panzer Grau). With its dark, sinister tones, it is easy to see why it is so commonly used onscreen and in video games. However, this is not really reflective of the reality of camouflage on German military equipment. Whilst Germany has many prescribed and standardised methods of camouflage used throughout the war, you can guarantee that some obscure variations will also appear. Therefore, I will endeavour to cover the norm rather than the rarities of German vehicle painting.

German camouflage paint went through far more variations than any of the other major belligerents of the Second World War. At the outbreak of hostilities, German vehicles were painted a very dark grey with a dark brown disruptive pattern. This pattern can be hard to spot in black-and-white photos, especially as the brown is fairly similarly dark to the grey. Whilst it may seem an odd choice of colour, especially given just how dark a grey was used, the intent appears to have been to provide a colour that would conceal the vehicle when it was parked in areas of shade.

By the summer of 1940, however – and probably earlier, as the German camouflage orders appear to typically postdate revisions to vehicle paint schemes – the brown part of the camouflage scheme was removed, and vehicles were finished simply in Panzer Grey.

Panzer Grey remained the norm into 1942, when some variation started to appear. With the German Army heavily committed to fighting in North Africa, a percentage of vehicles being produced were painted at the factory in a tan colour, RAL 8020 Gelbbraun. Being intended for use in tropical zones, when the German summer offensive began in the Southern Steppes of Russia and towards Stalingrad, many vehicles in this new paint colour were sent to Army Group South on the Eastern Front as well as North Africa. Notably, colour photos of Sturmgeschütz IIIs (StuG III) at Stalingrad are still extant. In addition to the Gelbbraun, German vehicles also began to have sand paint applied to between a third and a half of their surface, again, mostly in Army Group South.

In February 1943, the base colour of German vehicles was changed to RAL 7028 Dunkelgelb, with Olivgrün RAL 6003 and Rotbraun 8017 paints being issued for use for disruptive patterns. Dunkelgelb is best described as a sandy yellow colour, with a slightly green tint to it. Olivgrün is a medium green, roughly halfway between the brown and blue spectrum, and Rotbraun is, as the name suggests, a reddish brown colour.

Whilst the Dunkelgelb was applied at the factory, the green and brown were issued as tins of paste, with the camouflage to be applied by unit workshops, or even the vehicles' crews. As can be imagined, fairly extensive variations on these patterns exist, with irregular stripes or blotches of colours being the most common. On half to a third of the vehicles, a Dunkelgelb base is visible, with the remaining percentage of their surface being broken up with the disruptive scheme. Later in the war, especially as Germany lost the ability to contest the skies, heavier camouflage patterns were applied, with the Dunkelgelb being scarcely visible in some schemes. It was also possible for vehicles to have just one of the disruptive colours applied over the Dunkelgelb base.

As they were supplied as a paste, the green and brown paints could vary in colour and tone, depending both on how they were mixed and how they were applied, and appeared much darker in their undiluted form. They could be either sprayed onto the vehicle or applied with brush and broom, depending on the field conditions at the time.

It's worth noting that all of these camouflage patterns were intended for all German equipment, guns, soft-skins, tanks, half-tracks etc. Camouflage would typically only be applied to the exterior faces of vehicles such as half-tracks, armoured cars and trucks, and roofless cars with open passenger or load-carrying areas. The interior of an Sd.Kfz. 251 or *Kübelwagen*, for example, was Dunkelgelb. Fully enclosed vehicles, such as tanks, had their interiors painted ivory, although any interior faces of hatches were also painted Dunkelgelb.

In August 1944, the order was given for factories to apply camouflage paint to vehicles. This was intended to give greater uniformity and consistency to camouflage, as well as to significantly relieve the logistical and time constraints on workshop units. Each factory had its own pattern variations but generally, they were broad, typically hard-edged swathes of the vehicles' surface painted with large areas of the dark green and brown, with dots of Dunkelgelb applied to those areas to create the impression of light passing through trees. This came to be known as the *Hinterhalt* or Ambush pattern. The Ambush pattern camouflage scheme wasn't used for very long and was limited to armoured vehicles that were in production at that time. You don't tend to see it on guns, soft-skins, armoured cars or vehicles produced before August 1944.

In October 1944, new orders arrived for the paint schemes to change again. Due to ever-increasing shortages of paint, vehicles were still to be delivered in Ambush camouflage, but now with the red primer as the base, and then the green and sand colours painted over the top in a hard-edged pattern. The red primer was a reddish brown colour, a little lighter and redder than the Rotbraun used in the earlier camouflage patterns.

In November 1944, the situation changed again, with orders given for the base colour of vehicles to become RAL 6003 Olivgrün, again with Dunkelgelb and Rotbraun applied as camouflage. Most likely, these patterns were applied with a brush, as they too appear to be a hard-edged pattern.

Finally, in early 1945, the base tone reverted to Dunkelgelb. This could have been a retrospective change, however, as some factories perhaps continued using Dunkelgelb despite the previous changes. In the final few weeks of the war, as training schools were emptied of their vehicles, many of the more unusual prototypical and obsolescent ones were brought back into service, and often appear in either base Dunkelgelb or with some sort of hastily applied field camouflage.

Sometimes, German tanks have a gun barrel painted in a monochromatic colour that is distinctly different from the other tones on the vehicle when seen in black-and-white photographs. Most often, this is a replacement gun that is still in its primer colour. Unlike other components of the vehicle, however, German guns were painted with a heat-resistant grey primer. This was a much lighter tone than Panzer Grey, and was actually very close to modern-day grey primer.

The Germans made use of a temporary winter whitewash, as weather conditions required. This was typically applied all over the vehicle, to give a solid white finish, and was usually painted around tactical markings and numbers. As a temporary paint, it could quickly start to look a little worn and faded.

When it comes to German tactical markings, they again fall into a very general pattern, with lots of variation. In theory, an armoured vehicle would have a three-digit tactical number on the turret, or hull if it did not have a turret, and national markings on the sides and rear of the hull.

There would also usually be division markings on the front and rear of the vehicle.

The numbering system used by the Germans is, broadly speaking, pretty simple. These would be fairly large numbers, painted in black with a white outline. They took the form of company number, platoon number and individual vehicle number: 112, for example, would be from the first company, first platoon, and vehicle number 2. Whilst this is the theoretical case, many units adopted their own numbering systems, and especially for the outside of tanks, tended to either not use numbers or use single or double digits. Grossdeutschland Division also used a series of letters as well as numbers on their Tiger tanks, for example.

Colours for the numbers could also vary. Whilst white and black are the most common, red and white also appear. Pure black or white numbers are also seen, as are stencilled outlines or other colour variants.

National markings would take the form of a simple black-and-white cross, usually painted somewhere on either side of the hull, and somewhere on the rear plate, either above, between or next to the exhausts. Very late in the war, the white outline could be replaced with red. Also seen are simplified markings, utilising a black or white outline.

The division marking is normally painted on the front hull of the vehicle, and its position varied by division. This symbol was unique to its particular formation, and usually consisted of some sort of graphic or geometric shape. The Grossdeutschland Division, for example, used the stylised outline of a German helmet for its marking. It's worth searching for images of the particular formation you want to represent to see how they applied their markings.

Soft-skinned vehicles and often transports tended to be more simply marked; they usually just had a set of divisional markings and a number plate showing their branch of service: WH for the army, WL for the Luftwaffe, WM for the Kriegsmarine and SS runes for the SS.

The Germans did not particularly use camouflage netting on their vehicles but they did make heavy use foliage to conceal them. Stowage was generally limited to spare tracks, though StuGs would often have their engine decks covered in equipment as space inside the vehicle was restricted. Being largely on the defensive, there just wasn't a need for the Germans to carry as much stowage as their opponents did.

ZIMMERIT

Shortly after the Germans switched to using the three-tone camouflage, the surface of many armoured vehicles took on a corrugated appearance. This was actually a special type of paste named Zimmerit, used to prevent magnetic mines attaching to the vehicles. Zimmerit was a thick paste applied to tanks and assault guns from late 1943. The order for adding it to vehicles dated from December 1943, although it was applied to certain vehicles from the autumn. Germany had developed a magnetic anti-tank mine, which they introduced in 1943, and believed that the Allies would employ a similar weapon.

Application was predominantly limited to the following vehicle types: Panzer IV Ausf. H and early Ausf. J; Tiger I mid and late production; Panther Ausf. A and some Ausf. G; earlier King Tiger, especially those with the pre-production or Porsche turrets; the Sturmgeschütz III Ausf. G and Sturmgeschütz IV. Other vehicles to receive Zimmerit were the Sturmtiger, some Jagdtiger and some Jagdpanther. Of these vehicles, the variants mentioned are pretty much all likely to have had a Zimmerit application in one form or another. There were other types of vehicles and variants of the above that received Zimmerit, but they were far less common.

Application of Zimmerit stopped in September 1944, following concerns that it was flammable and likely to catch fire when shot at. Although testing refuted this, application was not resumed. This was probably because the Allies had not developed a magnetic anti-tank mine but also because the coating was time-consuming and expensive to apply, and added additional weight. The coating on a Tiger tank, for example, added an additional 200kg in weight.

Zimmerit was applied to vehicles in numerous patterns, although a series of vertical columns appears to be the most common variant and is seen on nearly all vehicles on which this product was used. It was applied to all vertical surfaces, and those surfaces that could be reached by infantry, although was not used on mudguards, fenders and *Schürzen* plates.

Making Zimmerit

Zimmerit paste is a detail you can add to vehicles if you wish. The vehicles most commonly associated with Zimmerit are variants manufactured between late 1943 and September 1944 (it was applied to some other vehicles, but rarely). These variants were as follows:

Vehicle type	Location covered
Sturmgeschütz III Ausf. G	Hull front, sides and rear. Not gun mantlet or *Schürzen* plates.
Panzer IV Ausf. H and early J	Hull front and sides (though not necessarily, if *Schürzen* present), rear hull, turret front.
Sturmgeschütz IV	Hull front, sides and rear. Not gun mantlet or *Schürzen* plates.
Brummbär	Hull front, sides and rear, although not applied to *Schürzen* or to gun mantlet.
Panther Ausf. A and early G	Hull front, sides and rear. Turret front sides and rear. Not applied to side skirts.
Jagdpanther (some vehicles)	Hull front, sides and rear. Zimmerit all the way up the sides of the vehicle, although not applied to gun mantlet.

Vehicle type	Location covered
Tiger I mid-production and late production variants (turrets with side-opening commander's hatch. Late also has steel wheels.)	Hull front, sides and rear. Turret front sides and rear. Not applied to side skirts.
Sturmtiger	Hull front, sides and rear, although only up as far as the armoured casemate.
King Tiger 'Porsche' turret version, and some production turret versions	All hull sides, as well as turret. Not applied to side skirts.
Jagdtiger, some early vehicles.	Applied to hull front, sides and rear, although only about halfway up the vehicle's superstructure.

Whilst it is not necessary to add for gaming use, it can be a nice detail to apply to models for a little extra authenticity, and is relatively simple, although time-consuming, to apply.

1 Prepare surface

Firstly, it is important to prepare the surface of the model for the application of the putty you will use to create the Zimmerit. This is because it may be a little smooth for the putty to properly adhere to, so you will need to add some texture. This is simply done by lightly sanding

the surface with some 600 to 800 grit wet and dry sandpaper. I always suggest using this product wet, to reduce dust and aid sanding.

2 Mix putty

There are many different putties on the market for modelling use. I prefer to use a two-part putty for making Zimmerit, as the drying times are long and it also bonds well with the model's surface. It's important to use a putty that is fairly thick and is robust enough to be pushed around and worked on. Here, I'm using Green Stuff, although Milliput and Tamiya two-part putty are also excellent products to use. Ensure that whichever putty you use is thoroughly mixed, otherwise it may not set properly. When it is properly mixed, it will be a solid colour without streaks.

3 Apply a thin layer of putty

Roll the putty into a sausage shape, and then lay it out in a layer on the model. You want to make this layer as thin as possible. It's also important to work in small areas. Do not try to cover the entire model in putty

in one go, as it will dry before you can get to work with it and you will definitely damage the putty in handling the model.

If the putty covers details, you can use a sharp knife to cut away any excess before you come to apply the texture.

4 Apply texture

There are numerous ways to apply texture to the putty. There are several tools available on the market in the form of stamps or scrapers that can be used to apply Zimmerit texture. It is also possible to use a knife blade or jeweller's screwdriver to press the pattern into the putty. My favourite method, though, is to use a razor saw dragged through the putty at an approximately 45-degree angle to the surface, for approximately 2 millimetres, and then removed. I then repeat the process and keep adding a series of vertical columns of texture to the surface until I reach the end of the armour panel. If there are areas of detail I can't reach with the saw blade, I use an old scalpel blade to score the pattern into them.

PAINTING GERMAN CAMOUFLAGE

With such a varied and complex array of camouflage finishes, it would require a book in itself just to cover all the techniques to paint their patterns. Instead, I will cover probably the most prevalent and representative pattern used for most of the war. All the techniques will apply to the other patterns, however, and if you want to use a hard-edge scheme, you can simply brush paint on the disruptive scheme or use a masking putty or fluid type product.

Whilst German camouflage can appear intimidating to apply without an airbrush, it is possible to replicate the sprayed-on effect by brush. It's also worth remembering that many of the patterns were not sprayed so can quite simply be replicated by just painting on the disruptive scheme.

NO AIRBRUSH METHOD

1 Spray black

The first step is to use a can of black spray primer. Apply this all over the model. Given the complexity of some German vehicles, it may be worth keeping the kit in sub-assemblies and leaving off *Schürzen* plates if the model has them, to ensure the paint gets into all the details.

Brush used	Paint
Aerosol can	Citadel Chaos Black

2 Spray sand

We will now spray what is known as a zenithal coat using a sand-coloured rattle can paint. This is where a spray can is held at about a 45-degree angle from the model to apply the paint. This has the end result of leaving the darkest recesses still black and the most prominent areas of the model with the strongest, most opaque tone.

Brush used	Paint
Aerosol can	Army Painter Skeleton Bone

3 First camouflage tones

To approximate a sprayed-on effect, use the same paint to build up layers of opacity. If you wish to replicate more of a lightly sprayed version of the camouflage pattern, you would only really need to do this step, without moving on to the next one.

Now to apply both the green and brown colours of the pattern; the green is an olive mid tone and the brown, a darker, reddish tone. Thin both of these until they are just slightly thicker than a wash, and then

using a stabbing motion, stipple the pattern in the shape you desire onto the vehicle.

Brush used	Paint
Size 2, make-up brush	AK 11309 RAL 6003 Olivgrün AK 11330 RAL 8017 Rotbraun

4 Add depth to camouflage

If you wish to enhance these camouflage colours, you can go back and stipple more of your thinned paint onto the previously applied pattern. It's worth ensuring the previous layer is at least touch-dry, as you could potentially damage the paint.

Brush used	Paint
Size 1, make-up brush	AK 11309 RAL 6003 Olivgrün AK 11330 RAL 8017 Rotbraun

5 Highlights

Next, apply a drybrush with a Dunkelgelb tone. This will serve to pull all the previously applied steps together and also give some light weathering. Where the camouflage paint was field applied, it tended to be less hardwearing than the base paint underneath, so could wear quicker than the underlying Dunkelgelb.

Be careful if your model has Zimmerit on it. Concentrate your drybrushing to the edges and details of the model. If you start picking up the Zimmerit too much, you will lose the effect of the camouflage as it will be lost in the overly enhanced texture effect. You are now ready to paint the tools and running gear and also add transfers and any further weathering.

Brush used	Paint
Size 12 flat	Vallejo 976 Buff

AIRBRUSH METHOD

1 Spray dark brown

We will start this model off by painting it with a dark brown colour. It's probably worth putting a grey primer on the model first, especially if you are working on a resin or metal kit, or if you will be using acrylic paints.

Give the model a solid, overall coat of dark brown. Any tone will do, but remember it will also be acting as a shade; something like the colour

of chocolate should be perfect. You could alternatively use a red primer, although that will be a little light to work as shadows.

Brush used	Paint
Sparmax Max-4	Vallejo 822 German Camouflage Black Brown

2 Spray Dunkelgelb

The next step is to apply a layer of Dunkelgelb. I'll be using a sand tone that has a slightly greenish tint. Lightly mist a coat all over the model and then spray the Dunkelgelb onto each panel and armour plate, building up increasing levels of opacity. As you build up the colour, you will see the tone start to shift until it has an overall solid appearance on the model, with pronounced details in the shadow areas.

Brush used	Paint
Sparmax Max-4	AK 11318 RAL 7028 Dunkelgelb

3 Highlight Dunkelgelb

This is an optional step but can add some visual interest to the model if you want it. Spray a light coating of a paler sand colour into the centre of armour plates, and onto and around details. Use a very light application; you do not want to create blobs of colour, as you are trying to create a subtle effect.

Brush used	Paint
Sparmax Max-4	Vallejo 976 Buff

4 Spray green camouflage

Although it doesn't particularly matter in which order the camouflage paints are applied, I prefer to start with the green. It's a lighter tone than the brown, so may be harder to spray over it if the paint you are using is lacking in a little opacity. Spray this onto the vehicle in thin, random lines. Test it first on some spare parts or plasticard to check you are able to spray consistent lines of the thickness you want before committing to painting the model. Keep the brush moving and just randomly build up a pattern that looks about right to the eye. The aim is to cover about 30 per cent of the vehicle's surface.

Brush used	Paint
Sparmax Max-4	AK 11309 RAL 6003 Olivgrün

5 Spray brown camouflage

Now add the brown part of the camouflage pattern by applying a reddish brown paint in thin lines to about 30 per cent of the vehicle. Again, first test the paint on something that isn't your nearly completed model.

Brush used	Paint
Size 1, make-up brush	AK 11330 RAL 8017 Rotbraun

6 Spray a light coat of base

This is another optional step but is a good way to seal and unify all the previously applied colours. Applying a misting of the original Dunkelgelb tone to the model will help to give the vehicle a more naturalistic effect and reduce any contrasts in tones that might appear a bit extreme. Apply the paint in light, misting layers, ensuring that it doesn't go on too thickly as there is a risk of it running and pooling into recesses.

Brush used	Paint
Sparmax Max-4	AK 11318 RAL 7028 Dunkelgelb

STOWED TOOLS

With the camouflage painted, it is now time to start picking out the details. This is also now the time to apply any transfers you want to use (the application of transfers will be covered in a later chapter).

The tools on German vehicles were often painted along with the rest of the vehicle, but picking them out in different tones adds a lot more visual interest to the model. There are a couple of ways of doing this: you can either paint the metal tools with black, Panzer Grey or an alternative tone of Dunkelgelb as well picking out the wood parts with a natural wood colour. Tow cables should be a dark metallic colour.

Most German vehicles had metal tracks, with rubber road wheels on all but the latest vehicles of the war. Vehicles based on late production Tiger I, King Tiger, and some Panthers and Panzer IV all had steel wheels, although they were the minority of those in service with the German military.

Tracks were steel, and very quickly took on a dark brown colour, with shiny metal areas where they contacted the ground as well as where the road wheels run along the inside of the track. These colours apply to spare track on the vehicle too, although you could also paint them the same colour as the rest of the vehicle.

TOOLS

Most of the tools on the vehicle will be metal, but some handles, such as those on gun cleaning rods, spades and jack blocks, will be natural wood. Metal tools, such as jacks, spade blades, fire extinguishers and so on, will be Dunkelgelb, or possibly Panzer Grey if you want to add some variety.

Simply pick out these areas with a suitable colour of paint. I've added a few suggestions in the table below.

Brush used	Paint
Size 1 Round	Valllejo 995 German Grey or 882 Middlestone for metal areas. Vallejo 976 for untreated wood, or 983 Flat Earth for treated wood.

PINWASHING AND FILTERS

Filter

For this model, I'm going to use a brown olive filter. This time, I'll be using a premixed enamel filter for a tone I find particularly complimentary to German camouflaged vehicles, regardless of which variant of the camouflage scheme you are working with, and whether you have used an airbrush or not. You can also mix your own filter, either using an acrylic or oil paint.

If using an acrylic filter, glaze the paint on in thin layers, without letting it get streaky or blotchy. If you see the paint starting to run, using a clean, damp brush you can simply lift the paint from the surface of the model. Whichever method you go for, use a large flat brush to apply a thin, even layer of filter all over the model, including any transfers. If the model has Zimmerit, be careful it doesn't settle too deeply into the grooves of the pattern, although it will also nicely accentuate this detail if applied evenly.

Brush used	Paint
Size 4 Round	AK 076 Dark brown filter for NATO

Panel lining

To further enhance the detail, we will apply what is known as a pinwash along the panel and hatch lines, as well as around details such as tools. Dark brown is a very good colour for this, and this process is best done using either an oil or enamel paint. If you have used an oil or enamel for the filter layer as well, it is worth giving the model twenty-four hours or more before you come back and start using more oil or enamel-based paints, as they can easily reactivate the paint in the filter.

Here, I'm using a ready mixed pinwash, and relying on capillary action to let the wash flow into details. Note, I'm not applying it to enhance the texture of the Zimmerit as this will make the model appear too dark, and the texture will be too pronounced.

Brush used	Paint
Size 2 round	AK 2071 Paneliner for brown and green.

Jagdpanzer 38(t) Hetzer. This vehicle has a late war olive green-based camouflage, with hand-painted disruptive patterns.

Jagdpanther. This vehicle has Ambush, or Hinterhalt*, camouflage.*

King Tiger. Note the simplified late war cross on the turret.

Pak.40 and Kübelwagen.

Panther Ausf. D. This vehicle is in two-tone camouflage, as seen on some Panthers at the Battle of Kursk.

Panzer IV Ausf. G. This vehicle is representative of most Panzer IV between 1943 and 1945.

Semovente 75/18. This Italian vehicle is painted using the same colours as the German tones.

6

Transfers

Using transfers or decals is an excellent way of adding some finesse to your models, as well as speeding up the modelling process so that you don't need to paint on numbers and tactical markings by hand. They can be a little tricky to apply if you are not used to them, but there are a few ways of making them look painted onto the surface of the vehicle.

The vast majority of transfers available are the waterslide variety. These are an image printed onto a carrier film and held on a sheet of paper. Once dampened, the bond is loosened and they can be slid from the backing paper onto the model itself.

Two problems occur more than others when applying transfers. The first is the transfer creasing or not conforming to the detail on the model. This is caused by the carrier film of the transfer not being able to settle into and around details. It is an especially pronounced problem on tight curves and uneven surfaces, such as a Zimmerit paste. There are numerous products to treat transfers to help them melt into detail on the model, but a simple way to get transfers to fit around tight curves is to cut small nicks into the carrier film. This should give the transfer a greater ability to settle into the necessary shapes. For uneven surfaces, you will need to ensure the transfer is properly pressed into the model by rolling a cotton bud over the detail and gently pressing it into the surface.

Silvering is the other major issue you can run into with transfers. This is where the transfer has small air pockets between the transfer and the surface of the model. Many sources recommend using a gloss surface if you are going to apply transfers, although this is not really necessary. The silvering is caused by a surface not being perfectly smooth under the transfer, so as long as you ensure the transfer is pressed down properly, it should eliminate silvering. There are additional techniques you can try that we will cover later in this chapter.

For best results, apply transfers after the basic painting is complete but before you do any weathering.

SIMPLE METHOD TO APPLY TRANSFERS

This is the most basic method of applying transfers and is a good foundation to work from with all other methods of applying them.

1 Soak the transfer

First, trim the transfer from the rest of the backing sheet. It is best to work one at a time rather than soaking the whole sheet in one go. Then dip the transfer in a bowl of warm water and lay it on a sheet of foam. After about thirty seconds, the transfer should be starting to move. Slide the transfer onto the model and then position it where you need it.

2 Set into position

Leave the transfer for five to ten minutes and then gently roll a cotton bud over it. Be careful not to move the transfer. You can then repeat rolling the cotton bud over the transfer and applying a little more gentle pressure with each pass. This will settle the transfer into the surface.

VARNISH SEALANT

If you are applying a longer transfer with some connecting carrier film between images, say on propaganda text on Russian vehicles or turret numbers for German tanks, you may be at risk of silvering. A simple remedy to this is to paint some medium or varnish under the transfer immediately before you apply it to the surface.

1 Prepare the surface

While the transfer is soaking, apply a small amount of acrylic gloss varnish or medium to the location where the transfer will be placed. Be careful how much you apply: too much and it will spill out and potentially harm your prepared surface.

Brush used	Product
Size 2 round	Windsor & Newton Galeria gloss

2 Position the transfer

While the varnish is still wet, place the transfer on top of it and then press down with a damp cotton bud. Dampening the cotton bud will allow you to mop up any excess varnish. Let it set for a few moments and then burnish the transfer onto the surface, being sure to clean up the excess varnish that is pressed out from between the transfer and the surface.

As the transfer and varnish dry, they should create a solid surface that will be protected from silvering. I would strongly suggest applying a flat coat to the model once the transfers are dry, although this is down to personal taste.

SETTING SOLUTIONS

There are many setting solutions for transfers on the market. Most consist of a setting solution and a solvent, but some comprise just a single setting solution. The two-part products, such as Micro Sol/Set and Ultra Decal Fix, tend to give better results. These products work by essentially fixing the transfer to the surface and then melting it slightly, causing it to shrink to the surface of the model. They are the best ways to get a painted-on look to transfers.

I Setting solution

Soak the transfer as previously described, and while it is soaking, add a little setting solution to the surface to which it will be applied. Then apply the transfer. Once you are happy with its position, carefully burnish it with a cotton bud. Apply another layer of setting solution and then leave it for approximately twenty minutes before proceeding to the next stage.

Brush used	Product
Size 2 round	Mig Ammo 2029 Ultra Decal Set I

2 Fixing solvent

Once the transfer has had some time to settle into position, we can now apply some solvent. Ensure you have done all the burnishing you need to do before you go on to this stage, as the transfer will be very delicate until it has fully cured.

Simply paint some of the fixative solvent over the transfer and leave it to dry for a few hours. As this product will be breaking down the transfer to the surface of the model, be careful you do not knock or touch it, as it can ruin it. In addition, some fixatives can be fairly strong and have the potential to impair the result. Whilst they are fine to paint onto the model, any sort of contact with them is likely to damage the underlying paint.

I'd also suggest giving the model a coat of matt varnish once the transfers are dried. This should give them a very pleasing painted-on appearance.

Brush used	Product
Size 2 round	Mig Ammo 2030 Ultra Decal Fix 2

These transfers have been sealed in with setting solution and then weathered with the rest of the model.

The complex shapes of this M8 Greyhound required significant burnishing into place to get the transfers to conform to the surface detail.

This M10 had its transfers sealed with varnish before being heavily weathered.

7

Stowage

Adding stowage is a great way to personalise your models. Stowage can represent anything from tarpaulins, food and supply crates, spare wheels and tracks, personal equipment belonging to the crew, fuel cans, tow cables, unhitching logs, and even spare transmissions or bicycles.

Typically, armies on the offensive would be carrying their supplies with them, whilst those on the defensive did not need to as they were not at risk of outstripping their supply lines. As such, Allied vehicles, especially Western Allied vehicles, tend to be quite heavily laden with stowage, with American equipment being the most likely to be loaded down. That's not to say, however, that Russian and German vehicles didn't carry stowage. Russian vehicles, particularly between the latter part of 1944 and the run to

Berlin, are quite often seen with equipment on their engine decks, although this space was still kept largely clear for supporting infantry to ride on. With the Germans, the Sturmgeschütz especially can be seen with a great deal of stowage, as there was so little storage space within the vehicle.

Whilst not necessarily stowage, sandbags can also be seen pressed into service as make-do additional armour. The actual level of protection this provided is open to debate, but it did give crews additional confidence in their equipment, if nothing else.

When adding stowage, be aware that whilst there is an element of placing it wherever it will fit, crew still needed to access hatches and fuel caps, as well as be able to fight from the vehicle. This means that vision and weapon placement must be kept clear of stowage. It's also worth thinking a little about how stowage is actually attached to the vehicle. Aside from the rear deck, there are rarely any flat areas that can have equipment attached to them on vehicles, unless the equipment is tied on in some way. Also, remember that equipment tied to the side is more likely to get snagged and caught, and therefore lost.

You can attach stowage at any part of the modelling process. My preference is to paint it separately and add it to the model once the vehicle itself is painted but before it is weathered.

PAINTING STOWAGE

With potentially so many different items on a vehicle, it is difficult to show every possible permutation that may be stowed. As such, this chapter will provide a starting-off point of colours and techniques to use. As a general rule of thumb, metalwork would be in the colour of the nation's standard equipment – Olive Drab, Dunkelgelb and 4BO Green, for example. Wooden areas would generally be a natural wooden tone, and either treated or untreated. Canvas equipment would be either an untreated buff or a khaki tone.

Painting tracks is covered elsewhere in this book, so does not need repeating here.

TARPS AND PACKS

These would be the colours of the nation's webbing, so most often, khaki and grey tones are appropriate. We will use some basic figure painting techniques. How much detail you want to go into is entirely up to you, but I prefer to keep the painting fairly simple.

1 Khaki base tone

Firstly, apply a neat, even coat of a suitable colour for the equipment. As this is going to be on an American vehicle, we will paint it with khaki. This may require more than one coat, so be prepared to do a few thin coats to ensure you have a neat and opaque base.

Brush used	Paint
Size 1 round	Vallejo 988 Khaki

2 Shading wash

To add more visual interest to the stowage, now add a shading wash. Greens, browns and greys are all excellent choices of colour here, and you could use a couple to add some visual variation to the stowage. On these pieces, I've used a light brown shade on some items and an olive green tone on others, but feel free to experiment and see what you like the look of.

Brush used	Product
Size 2 round	Army Painter Strong Tone Army Painter Military Shader

3 Highlight step

This is an optional step but can serve to make the detail on the stowage really pop. You can either paint on the highlights as if you were working on a figure, or drybrush the detail on. To illustrate both effects, the pack on the left has painted-on highlights, whilst the one on the right has drybrushed highlights.

Brush used	Product
Size 1 round Size 2 flat	Vallejo 987 Medium Grey

CRATES

Wooden crates were used for storing all manner of items. These could be made from treated or untreated wood, and came in a variety of brown shades. They could even be painted in the colours of the nation's vehicles. Here, I am painting a simple neutral wooden tone onto the box, but you can use any method of painting brown that you like.

1 Grey base tone

To get a worn and untreated look to the wood, we will use a neutral, medium grey for the base colour. You could equally use ochres and buff tones, or even shades of brown.

Brush used	Product
Size 1 round	Vallejo 987 Medium Grey

2 Dark brown shade

You can add a wash or thinned layer of paint over the base. However, the recent creation of contrast and speed paints has made adding shade and texture to items with high texture, such as wooden objects, very easy.

Select a tone that you feel fits the look you want to achieve and apply a layer of the paint, using your brush to lift it if it is a little too thick or it starts to pool. These types of paints can be quite hard on a brush, so it's worth using an older brush rather than your best one. You could add some drybrushing of the base tone, but I like how the crate appears as it is.

The crate on the bottom has been drybrushed with the base tone as a comparison.

Brush used	Paint
Size 2 round	Citadel Contrast Wyldwood

FUEL AND AMMUNITION CANS

Fuel cans, or jerry cans, as well as ammunition boxes for small arms, would generally be made of metal and painted in the same colours as any other metal equipment for their parent nation. It was not uncommon to use captured jerry cans, and this can be a nice way of adding some extra visual interest to a model. Jerry cans would also be used for transporting drinking water. These were typically marked out with a white cross, either across the centre of the can, similar to a Balkenkreuz, in the case of German jerry cans, or a white X in the stamped recesses in American cans.

Here, we will do one German and one American jerry can. The processes will be the same for both, so I will call out relevant changes to the base tones, but all other steps will be identical.

1 Base tones

For the German can, use the same Dunkelgelb we have used in painting the rest of the vehicle, although you could also have an older can in Panzer Grey, if you wish. For that, you will need a very deep dark grey.

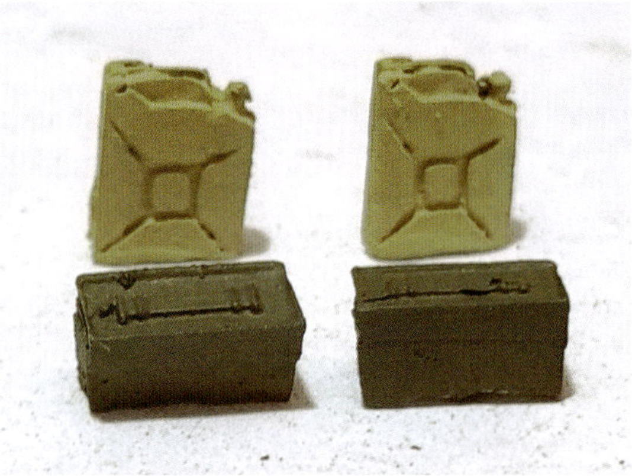

For an American or British-supplied can, I'll use an olive tone. For a bit of variation, though, I am using a slightly different shade of green. Apply an even coat of colour – you can either brush on or airbrush the paint, as you prefer. I've used a brush for simplicity.

Brush used	Paint
Size 2 round	AK 11318 Dunkelgelb AK 11156 Camouflage Green

2 White cross

Should you wish to designate a can for use with drinking water, paint a white cross or X on both sides of the body, depending on where it came from. German cans have the cross on the centre of the body; Allied ones have it in the stampings of the body, as shown in the images.

The best way to get neat lines is to paint one continuous line, let it set, then go back over it to improve opacity. You can always come back with your base tone to neaten up any slippage.

Brush used	Paint
Size 1 round	AK 11001 White

3 Panel lining

We will enhance the detail with an enamel wash, although you could use any preferred method of adding a wash to the model as the process will be much the same, except if you are working with acrylics, when you will need to be a bit quicker.

Apply a dark greenish brown wash all over the jerry can and then remove the excess wash with a cotton bud. With an acrylic, remove the wash pretty much as soon as it's applied. With an enamel or oil wash, let the paint become touch-dry and then remove it with a cotton bud soaked in thinners.

Brush used	Paint
Size 2 round	AK 2071 Paneliner for brown and green

This Sherman has had sandbags added to it. They were simply made from rolling green stuff into a sausage, then cutting to length and placing on the vehicle. They were painted using the methods detailed for canvas and tarpaulins.

L3000 Mercedes. You can use stowage to create a narrative in your models, such as this truck loaded with fuel supplies.

M10 tank destroyer. Not all stowage has to be military in nature, such as the milk churn hanging from the back of this vehicle.

8

Weathering

Weathering is a bit of a catch-all term for applying varying degrees of ageing and lived-in effects to a model. There are many methods of weathering, from simply applying a little light patina to areas that tarnish naturally, such as tracks and exhausts, to full-on, caked-on mud and grime.

Personally, I prefer to add weathering once the model has had its stowage added and painted, as well as transfers applied, but before any crew models are added. It's best to think of it as the final stage of the model. Much of this is entirely down to personal taste. Some people prefer immaculate, fresh-from-the-factory looking models, whereas others like their models to look more used, whilst still others prefer models to look absolutely worn and beaten up.

There is no right or wrong way to apply weathering, as all approaches represent a different stage of a vehicle's life. If you want to take a more historical approach to your models, it's worth taking a look at photos from the theatre, campaign or even unit you are intending to reproduce at the time these machines were operational.

There is a surprising number of images available from even a simple internet search that can help you achieve a realistic level of weathering on your models. In Normandy, for example, the majority of vehicles were brand new, or drawn from training schools and refurbishment, so tended to be lightly weathered at the start of the campaign – being pretty much restricted to some dust. However, a few months later, at the end of the campaign, vehicles tend to look much more worn, with scratched and scuffed paint, layered mud and even missing mudguards.

Military vehicles, especially those in a combat zone, have a tendency to get filthy very quickly. Mud and dust can soon accumulate. In hot, dry weather, vehicles, especially tracked vehicles, tend to gain layers of dust that can rapidly lighten the underlying paint. Conversely, in wet and wintery weather, mud will cover it equally quickly, being thrown up by tyres or tracks as it moves, and also transported into the vehicle as its crew enters and maintains the machine. Grease accumulates around working parts, and layers of dust tend to highlight any fuel and oil spills that occur during maintenance. You can often see dark stains around filler caps, wheel bolts and bearings.

Battle damage is quite a popular effect to add to vehicles, although is generally best kept at a subtle level for realism, at least for a vehicle that is still combat operational. Good ways to represent combat damage are to damage fenders, add soot marks, and leave off parts like *Schürzen* on German vehicles. Rust can give a nice effect, but should be used sparingly. An average combat vehicle, such as a tank, did not have a particularly long service life, and would have been maintained between major operations. That said, rust does tend to accumulate on areas that generate a lot of heat, such as exhaust pipes, and is especially notable on some German and Russian vehicles.

Areas such as grab handles and chipped paint may exhibit some surface rust but are more likely to have a darker, more worn metal appearance. This will look more like a shiny brown where the metal has tarnished, although could also be the primer paint showing through.

Paint, especially matt paint, will fade and discolour depending on the local weather conditions as well as the general use and damage the surface may receive. This has the effect of creating subtle changes in tone on the vehicle's surface. Additionally, rain can lead to further discolouration, either through cleaning off surface dust or carrying dirt from other parts of the vehicle. Both of these can make for interesting and varied effects and add a lot of visual interest to the model's surface.

Tracks, regardless of material, nation, or how they were treated before being fitted or issued to vehicles, tended to be a dark brown colour, as their metal oxidised and their primers and preservative paints quickly eroded. Areas where the track contacted the ground quickly take on a shiny silver colour. It's worth pointing out that some tracks, particularly those used on a few Sherman variants, had rubber contact pads and so didn't get this shiny appearance. It's also worth ensuring that you pick out the guide horns and inner faces of any tracks in silver as this will represent their contact with the road wheels.

Whilst dirt frequently builds up on tracks, when adding earth and ground effects to them, it's a good idea to keep the areas where the track actually contacts the ground a brighter silver, and then adding areas of thicker mud and grass to deeper parts of the external side of the track. Given the constant movement of track, the inner facings tend to stay pretty shiny and clean.

I'll use an American Sherman for most of the guides here, but all of the techniques apply to any nation's vehicles, and most colours also apply. I'll call out any differences where necessary.

The next stage is to paint the tracks, distressing the paint, adding dust and grime, and creating thick mud as well as some rust effects. Not all of these techniques will be relevant for every model, but this will give you a tool set to choose from when working with your projects.

TRACKS

For this particular Sherman, we have dark metal tracks, with rubber pads. This only really applies to some vehicles with Sherman and Grant chassis, as well as some German half-tracks.

1 Brown base paint

Firstly, add a layer of dark brown paint to both sides of the track, ensuring all areas are covered. This may require two coats. It's important to thin your paint so that it will flow into the details, but be careful you do not over-thin the paint in case it floods or spatters onto areas you've already painted.

This won't apply to most vehicles, but if you haven't done so already, you can also use this colour to pick out the tyres with the same paint. Use a very dark grey paint, though not black, for rubber areas. Pure black looks a little too dark for natural rubber, especially at the scales of model we are working with. Naturally, this also applies to adding tyres to wheeled vehicles.

Brush used	Paint
Size 3 round	Vallejo 822 German Camouflage Black Brown
Size 3 round	Vallejo 862 Black Grey

2 Worn metal

Now we can pick out the areas that would wear and be free of tarnishing. I'm going to use a gunmetal tone for these areas, and on the Sherman, I'll apply the metal tone to the inside of the tracks as well as to the teeth on the drive sprocket. If you have a vehicle with metal tracks, you can also drybrush them to enhance the detail. Metallic paints can be a little lacking in opacity, so this stage may require more than one layer

Brush used	Paint
Size 2 round	Citadel Leadbelcher
Size 2 flat for drybrushing	Citadel Leadbelcher

3 Dust

This is an optional step, but if you want to begin making the vehicle appear a little more used, you can add a layer of dust to the whole of the vehicle's running gear and suspension. Even if you are intending to add further dirt and grime to the model, this is still a good starting point. Here, I've used a premixed enamel wash, although you can use any method of applying a thin wash if you prefer using a light buff tone.

We will apply the wash all over the relevant areas of the vehicle, including the sides, rear and front of the hull if you wish. While the paint is still wet, lift it from the surface of the model, without allowing it to pool or become too thick.

Brush used	Paint
Size 2 round	AK 074 Rainmarks

PAINT CHIPPING AND DISTRESSING

As the paint on a vehicle is battered and used, it will gradually start to gain chips and scratches as well as localised discolouration. These are relatively simple effects to replicate but can add a lot of detail to the finish of a model. I prefer to apply these steps by doing the discolouration of the paint first before applying chipping, This allows you to use techniques that are potentially damaging to underlying paint without harming the more delicate effect of chipping.

1 Discolouration

This stage does really require the use of enamel or oil paints as it involves subtle blending of paints. Acrylics dry too quickly and also have a tendency to not remove as easily as we need them to.

We will use several different oil paints and apply tiny dots of browns, buff and grey tones to all the surfaces on the model. This will look completely wrong and unnatural, but that will be fixed in the next stage.

Brush used	Paint
Size 2 round	Windsor & Newton Payne's Grey
	Windsor & Newton Naples Yellow
	Windsor & Newton Indian Yellow

2 Blending

Next is to blend and feather the dots until they are almost invisible, just leaving a faint trace of pigment on the surface. For a more weathered effect, you can adjust how much of the paint you blend out. Dip a medium-sized make-up brush in some white spirit or odourless thinner, dry it with some kitchen paper, and then start to blend out the spots with vertical movements of the brush on the sides and a stippling motion on the top of the model.

Brush used	Product
Medium make-up brush	White spirit or odourless thinner

3 Chipping and scratches, light tone

Chipping and scratches are relatively simple to add to a model and can really enhance the impression of wear and use. You'll need some sponge (the stuff from figure cases or blister packs is ideal), a lighter version of the base colour of your vehicle, such as a very pale green or ivory, as well as a dark brown. You can use these tones individually or together, as I will do here, to get more texture onto the model.

The easiest way of keeping your chipped paint looking irregular is to dip some of the sponge in your light paint and then dab it along the areas of wear. Changing the orientation of the sponge can help to create an irregular appearance. To add scrapes, rather than chips, drag the sponge along the surface of the model to create a fine, ragged line.

Apply the chipping to areas that will draw in the most significant areas of wear, such as around hatches, front of the hull, and edges of the vehicle.

Brush used	Paint
Sponge section	Vallejo 885 Pastel Green

4 Dark chipping

If you want to add some more wear to your chipping, you can apply some dark brown to represent the underlying surface of the vehicle, as well as add a more three-dimensional effect to any chipping. Apply these in and around the lighter chips. You can either paint them into some of the light-toned chips, or again use a sponge around the previously applied tones to add the extra level of weathering.

Brush used	Paint
Sponge section	Vallejo 882 German Camouflage Black Brown

DUST AND DIRT

1 Dust base tone

At this point, we can now start to distress the paint on the vehicle. There are two ways to do this, depending on the level of weathering and appearance you want. Following on from the previous layer of dust on the tracks, we will apply some dust to the upper areas of the vehicle. Again, use an enamel wash, although you could use oil or clay washes. Whilst you can do these techniques with acrylics, it's a much greater level of work and there is more risk of the effect failing, or at least not coming out as well as you would like.

This tank is intended to replicate the appearance of a vehicle with a significant layer of dust on operation in the Normandy campaign, so I will apply some dust around the lower areas on the sides of the hull, the bottom edges of armour plates and turret sides, and near any hatches and other flat areas. It's important not to let the paint go into any of the deep cracks and joins of the armour plates, although these can always be tidied up later. I prefer to use a stippling method and an older brush to apply this effect, as it gives a more uneven, irregular finish, which looks more natural. I've also applied some vertical lines to represent dust that has been affected by rain and water dripping from the vehicle.

Brush used	Paint
Size 2 round	AK 074 Rainmarks

2 Dust blending

Working quickly, once the paint has become touch-dry, we can now blend the paint applied in the previous step. Using a soft, rounded brush, lightly damped in thinners, we will soften the edges of the areas of dust. For the vertical streaks, use the same technique to blend most of the paint into the surrounding area using up and down strokes of the brush. Depending how worn you want the vehicle to look, to achieve more prominent streaks, blend the paint less. Blending the paint more will give you a subtler effect.

You can also do this with acrylics, but you will have to work with the paint while it is still wet and in much smaller areas, say one side of the vehicle at a time, and use water or medium to blend the paint.

Brush used	Product
Size 2 round	White spirit or odourless thinner

3 Adding depth

These next few stages are optional but can be a good way to add additional depth and interest to the colours. Here I am using enamels, although any other paints can be used, with the limitations to acrylics already mentioned.

This time, we will add a darker brown with an earthy tone to the areas we have already painted with the dust colours. This could represent damp areas of dust, or thicker, fresh areas that have not dried out yet.

You can either apply the dark tone while the lighter one is still wet, or leave it to dry overnight before coming to this step. If you apply it while both paints are wet, they will blend into a more naturalistic effect, but might be too subtle to see the distinction. My preference, as I have done here, is to leave the paint overnight to dry, and then apply the earth tone.

Again, stipple the paint on, applying it to the lower and densest areas of dust. I recommend doing this to the tracks and suspension too.

Brush used	Paint
Size 2 round	AK 4063 Brown Earth Deposit

4 Blending earth tone

If we were to blend the paint as we did in Step 2 in adding the dust effects to the model, we would risk removing some of the work we have already done. Instead, just apply some thinner to the edges of the earth paint and allow the properties of the thinners to help the two paints blend naturally. Given the nature of what we are trying to achieve, it does not need to be a smooth blend, it just needs to get rid of the effect of two paints on top of one another.

Brush used	Product
Size 2 round	White spirit or odourless thinner

5 Grease and fuel spills

This is another optional step and can be a nice way of adding some extra signs of use. A few dark black or brown patches and streaks can really enhance the look and realism of a model, despite also being very simple to apply. Ideally, you will have been able to leave the dust effects to dry overnight before working this stage.

We will again use an enamel wash product, this time a dark, somewhat indeterminate greenish, brownish sludge colour. You can, of course, mix one instead if you prefer.

Apply some vertical lines to the sides of the hull and turret, and blend them in the same way as we did with the dust effects. This will add further subtle discolouration to the vehicle, suggestive of rain or grime being washed off.

For the fuel and grease spills, apply the paint around the fuel filler caps on the engine deck in fairly random patterns to replicate drips and spills, and you can also apply the same paint around the bolts and hubs of wheels to show where grease has been added to the suspension. Once the dark tone is in place, gently dab the edges with a brush that has been dampened with thinners to give a feathered finish.

Brush used	Paint
Size 2 round	AK 2071 Paneliner for Brown and Green

WET MUD

To create more of a wet mud effect, say for vehicles operating in the autumn or winter, I recommend starting with the methods used in the dust stage, to build up an initial level of weathering. However, the big difference is that we will add some much thicker mud to the model, as well as some spatters of wet mud.

1 Thick mud

Now to add some texture paint around the running gear and lower hull of the vehicle. Areas that are moving parts, such as tracks and wheels, actually do not require as much of this effect, although you can still add some. Remember, as the vehicle is moving forwards, the mud is thrown up at the rear, so the back half of the vehicle is likely to have a heavier concentration of dirt than the front.

To create the mud, mix some Vallejo texture paint with some static grass. This gives the effect of thick soil and tufts of grass sticking to the vehicle. Apply some of the dark texture paint to a palette and add some static grass. For 28mm vehicles, I recommend 6mm static grass. For smaller sizes, 4mm or 2mm grass works well. Mix in as much as you feel is appropriate for the effect you want. Then, using an old brush, apply the mixture to the sides of the hull behind the running gear and to the rear of the hull. You can also add some to the wheels and tracks, although I recommend removing some of this paint with a cotton bud, leaving the texture paint in the recesses.

It's important to use an old paintbrush for this, as the microbeads in the texture paint will damage paintbrushes to the point where they can't be used again for fine work.

Brush used	Paint
Old size 2 round	Vallejo 218 Dark Earth texture paint

2 Brown base tone

We will now apply a brown, earthy tone. My preference here is to use an enamel product, although you can get much the same effect with a suitable acrylic colour. I've painted this all over the running gear, lower hull and tracks, and stippled it along the sides and rear of the tank, as well as anywhere that would naturally attract dirt, including places where the crew may be boarding the vehicle and carrying mud on their boots.

Brush used	Paint
Size 2 round	AK 4063 Brown Earth Deposit

3 Wet mud areas

The next stage is to apply some dark brown into areas that have a layer of texture paint. This will create the effect of the mud being fresh and damp, as if it has recently been pulled by the vehicle as it moves.

Mix a thin layer of dark brown oil paint – although if you are using acrylics, you can achieve the same effect with thinned paint. Simply paint this onto the texture areas, then stipple it at the edges so that it blends with the underlying layer. If you are using oils and enamels, the paints will naturally blend together without requiring any additional work.

Brush used	Paint
Size 2 round	Windsor & Newton Raw Umber

4 Mud spatter

To create the effect of wet mud being thrown up onto the vehicle from puddles, we can very simply flick some buff-coloured paint onto the vehicle. Again, I'm using an enamel as it is easy to clean up and remove if it doesn't look right, but you can achieve the same effect with acrylic.

Load some paint onto a flat, dry brush and then remove any excess so that it is holding a minimal amount of paint. This is important to ensure control over the flow of paint in the next step.

With a cocktail stick in one hand and the model propped up so that each surface is roughly at a right angle to you, flick the brush

against the cocktail stick. This will spatter the paint onto the vehicle and give a convincing effect of having been moving through mud in bad weather.

Brush used	Paint
Size 2 flat	AK 4062 Light Dust Deposit

RUST

Whilst surface rust would be rare on these vehicles, it could occur along areas where paint has been damaged, and especially to exposed exhausts, such as those found on some Russian and German vehicles.

Fresh rust has a fairly bright orange tone and then darkens down as it ages. It is also notable for having numerous colours present, ranging from greys to oranges to browns, as well as having different textures. Given the size of some of the parts we will be working on, we need to overemphasise this effect somewhat, although as with everything in this book, the techniques should be used as a starting-off point and you can then experiment with your own choices of paint.

I will also demonstrate techniques for using both enamels and acrylics, although my personal preference is for enamels.

1 Grey base tone

Initially, the area to be painted with the rust is given a light to medium grey base colour. Rust often has grey tones to it, and working from a

solid, neutral base like this will give you an authentic looking finish. This is suitable for both acrylic and enamel methods.

Brush used	Paint
Size 2 round	Vallejo 987 Medium Grey

ACRYLIC METHOD

1 Orange brown base tone

To get an uneven, realistic texture to your rust effect, we need to mix the paint with some water to make it much thinner. However, we will not be using it as a wash, so don't thin it quite that much. The next stage is to stipple an orange-brown tone all over the exhaust. To create a rust streak, I have also painted on a thin line of the same orange-brown and then feathered it as soon as it is applied to give a subtle rust streaking effect.

Brush used	Paint
Size 2 round	Vallejo 981 Orange Brown

2 Stipple on medium brown

Using an older brush, next stipple on a medium reddish brown. The intent here is not to obscure the orange or grey tones but to add extra texture to them. You can use the paint either significantly thinned, as with the orange-brown, or straight from the pot. I've used the paint straight from the pot to add further contrast to the surface.

Brush used	Paint
Old size 1 round	Vallejo 940 Saddle Brown

3 Stipple on dark brown

As in Step 2, now we can add some further texture to the rust using a very dark brown. Use the paint straight from the pot and lightly stipple it onto the surface. You do not need much of it to have a very noticeable effect on the rust surface.

Brush used	Paint
Old size 1 round	Vallejo 822 German Camouflage Black Brown

ENAMEL METHOD

1 Light Rust

I find the enamel process is much easier and quicker than using acrylics. From the same acrylic grey base, apply three tones and leave them to dry. As enamels have a much longer drying time compared to acrylics, you can layer each of the paints used on top of one another while they are still wet; they will diffuse and blend together via capillary action to give you a very nice, realistic effect.

Firstly, stipple on a fairly heavy layer of Light Rust. You can use these products straight from the pot and do not need to thin them. Remember that enamels require cleaning in spirits or odourless thinner.

Brush used	Paint
Old size 1 round	AK 4111 Light Rust Deposits

2 Medium Rust

Whilst the previous layer is still wet, we will now use the same stippling motion to add the next level of texture to the rust. This time, the rust product is a brownish orange, and we can just stipple it on over the top of the previous paint.

Brush Used	Paint
Old size 1 round	AK 4112 Medium Rust Deposits

3 Dark Rust

Finally, stipple on a darker brown tone. This will really serve to bring out the texture of the rust and make it look good. The photos show the final effect of the rust once it has dried. The good thing about enamels is that if at any stage you aren't happy with the effect, you can wipe them off with a cotton bud, or a brush soaked in white spirit or odourless thinners. This is also a good tone to use for rust streaks. I've painted a small dot onto the model and then used a dry brush to simply drag the paint down to create a streak of rust.

Brush used	Paint
Old size 1 round	AK 4113 Dark Rust Deposits

BATTLE DAMAGE

Whilst serious battle damage would render a vehicle combat ineffective, some elements can really add to the detail and character of a model.

Most vehicles had some form of sheet or thin metal covering over parts of the tracks, as well as the stowage bins on hulls and turrets being made from thin metal. These parts have a tendency to either fold or crumple and can also dent easily. This is best applied when you are still assembling the model.

Schürzen plates on German vehicles tended to get knocked off rather than become deformed, as they were simply held on to the vehicles with hooks. The extra turret *Schürzens* on the Panzers III and IV, though, were solid plates welded to the vehicle and do not generally show much sign of damage.

Here, I will demonstrate removing a fender and adding dents to the fuel cells of a T-34 tank. You can use these techniques to modify further any other areas of the vehicle, as well as different types of vehicle.

DENTED METAL

Firstly, assemble the part and ensure all the glue is dry and seams are cleaned up. Then, using a needle file, sand in the effect of the dent. You can use any shape of file you like, depending on the particular shape of the dent you want to add. Here, I've used a round file, and sanded in a few dents into the part. Make a note of the thickness of the plastic, however, and ensure you do not sand straight through it.

REMOVING FENDERS

Removing fenders is a very quick but effective way of adding some battle damage to a model. Have a look at reference photos to see how the particular vehicle you are modelling weathered and took damage, and then simply use some sprue cutters to clip off the relevant area. You can then tidy up the area with files to get a neat break. On this T-34, I have removed both the front fenders, although you could also only remove one for a more asymmetrical appearance.

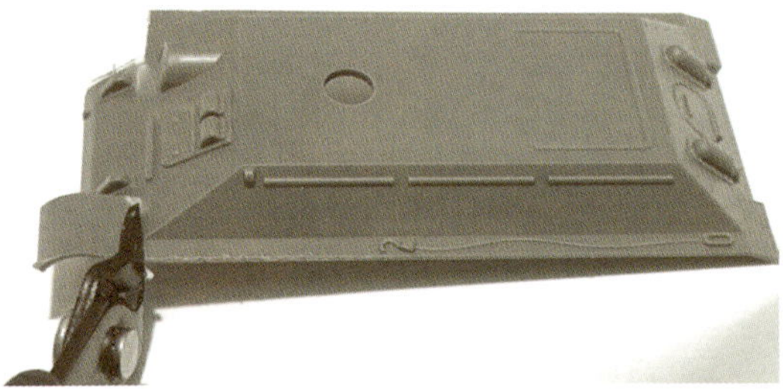

Sd.Kfz.251 Ausf. D. This vehicle has had one of its stowage hatches opened.

Mercedes L3000.

Panther Ausf. D.

Panzer IV Ausf. H. This vehicle has heavy chipping along the sides of its Schürzen *plates.*

M4A1 Sherman. The heavy dust effects were created by building up successive layers of dust, streaking and blending.

T-70.

Detail on the T-70 tracks, demonstrating the different textures achieved with the techniques in this chapter.

9

Foliage and Camouflage

Concealing and disguising equipment to prevent the enemy knowing your actions has been an integral part of warfare for millennia. Armoured vehicles were no exception, especially with the growing effectiveness of aerial reconnaissance and attacking capability, rendering movement without air superiority very dangerous to any vehicle.

The Western powers, especially the British, often used camouflage netting to disguise vehicles, whereas the Russians and Germans heavily camouflaged their machines with tree branches and foliage. The Western Allies also made use of foliage, particularly in tank destroyer units. British vehicles had netting laced with hessian strips, whilst American equipment used a fairly standard net. British vehicles, especially, can be seen with the netting over their turrets, although the Americans seem to have used it more on the hull than the turret.

Foliage can be a little delicate on models, but if you are careful how you position it, it can work very well and still be quite robust. Nets, on the other hand, are nicely resilient to handling and use on the gaming table.

It's worth bearing in mind that most foliage would be removed from a vehicle before going into action, although some typically remained attached to the sides and rear, where it would not block vision and access to the vehicle.

Whilst you could just glue clumps of flock onto a model, this tends to look like you've just glued clumps to the model. Modelling lichen is another option but it is quite delicate, and once it dries out it will become brittle and fall apart. Instead, my preference is to use seafoam. You can buy springs of this from most online retailers, and it comes in fairly large packs. It is already dried out and although quite fine, once coated with PVA glue it becomes surprisingly robust. I'll demonstrate two different methods for using this product, the first for evergreen leaves and the second for deciduous leaves.

It is strongly recommended to wait until the model is almost finished before adding any foliage to it. My preference is to add it as the final step before giving the model a flat coat.

DECIDUOUS FOLIAGE

When making foliage, I like to take a piece of seafoam, add leaves to it, and then give this a wash of some green or brown paint. Once fully dried, I cut the parts into suitably sized branches and attach them to the model.

1 PVA coating

To begin with, we will give our seafoam a coating of PVA glue. This serves two purposes. Firstly, it allows us to attach the leaves to the branches.

Perhaps more importantly, as PVA dries it will form a rubbery texture around the branches and make them considerably more resilient. Dilute the PVA with water. To apply the glue, it is best to use a fairly large, flat brush.

Brush used	Product
Size 8 flat	PVA glue

2 Adding leaves

While the PVA is still wet, tip some of the modelling leaves into a small bowl, and then sprinkle a handful or so onto each branch until the density of the leaves builds up to the level you want. When working in 15mm, you may want less density than in 20mm or 28mm. A quick internet search should reveal an extensive array of leaves. You will want to find some as close to the scale of your model as possible. Luckily, between the scale modelling and model railway communities, most popular wargaming sizes are also covered.

Once you are happy with the density of the leaves, set aside the seafoam tree to dry. I'd recommend at least overnight to allow it to fully harden.

3 Brown wash

With the leaves fully dried, you can apply a wash if you wish to. This will help to tie them in to the finish of the model, as well as unify the colours between the branches and the leaves. For a more aged look, use a brown wash; for fresher leaves, use a green one, ideally an olive tone.

Brush used	Paint
Size 8 flat	Army Painter Soft Tone or Army Painter Military Shader

EVERGREEN FOLIAGE

Naturally, vehicles tend to be camouflaged to fit with their surrounding environments. When using foliage, this requires using branches cut from local flora. For vehicles operating in the Battle of the Bulge, for example, you would see branches from fir trees used as additional camouflage. This is a distinctive look but requires the same techniques as making deciduous branches. This process is largely the same as with the deciduous foliage, but there are two distinctions.

1 Adding needles

To add needles to the branches, we can use essentially the same process as before. Coat the branches with PVA, but instead of adding leaves, we are using static grass. For this, I'd recommend either 2mm or 4mm products, and in a fairly dark green

colour. Instead of sprinkling them onto the model, you may need to apply the foliage as a pinchful to achieve a greater density of foliage.

2 Dark green wash

To replicate the darker tone of evergreens, once the previous step has been done and the model is fully dry, we will give the parts a green wash. If you have a fairly dense product, it may be worth thinning the wash with water a little. Once the wash has dried, use the same process to apply the branches as with the deciduous foliage.

Brush used	Paint
Size 8 flat	Army Painter Green Tone

ATTACHING BRANCHES

Using sharp scissors cut the sea foam into suitably sized branches. There's no hard and fast rule to this, but I tend to go with what looks like the size of branch the average person could easily cut and lift into place on the vehicle. Once you have a small pile of branches, pick them up with

tweezers, dip them into PVA on a palette, carefully ensuring that the glue is confined to the surface that will be in contact with the model. You can then place the branch onto the model.

Repeat this process until you have the desired amount of camouflage on your vehicle.

CAMOUFLAGE NETTING

We can now look at adding camouflage nets to a model. There are many commercially available camouflage nets for scale modelling, or you can use medical gauze. They are largely the same, except the modelling products have usually already been dyed green and brown tones. Here, I will be using a green toned camouflage net I found on eBay, although any similar product works; the process is exactly the same.

You can apply the netting to the model either before or after it is painted. Here, I am attaching it to an already painted model as I find the netting gets in the way of later adding transfers and weathering.

1 Shaping the net

The camouflage nets or gauze are supplied in fairly big sheets. I like to cut them into smaller pieces using sharp scissors. How big depends on the model you are intending to cover, but bear in mind that these nets were pretty big and could cover an entire hull or turret. I like to cut enough so that you could cover either the turret, gun barrel, or a side of the vehicle with it.

2 Attaching the netting

Attaching the netting is very simple. Dilute some PVA glue with water and paint it all over the net as if it were a wash. The net can then be folded and draped over the model in a way that looks realistic and natural. As a guide, there are many images available in books and online of how the actual vehicles were camouflaged with netting.

Brush used	Product
Size 8 flat	PVA glue

3 Add hessian strips

If you are modelling a British vehicle, you can add some hessian strips to the camouflage if you wish. Masking tape cut into strips about 2mm wide at most, and maybe several millimetres long, will be ideal. Once you have cut the masking tape into strips, you can attach it to the netting using PVA. Apply the strips roughly equidistant over the netting, then leave to dry overnight.

4 Brown wash

With the netting dry, carefully paint a dark brown wash over it. You can use either a premixed wash, a contrast-style paint, or thinned conventional paint, as long as it is a fairly dark brown tone. Capillary action should carry the paint throughout the netting surface. If you see the paint spilling onto the painted areas of the model, you can quickly lift it from the surface with a paintbrush.

A large brush is being used in this step as it has a significant well of paint, and this will ensure a consistent opacity to the wash across the netting.

Brush used	Paint
Size 4 round	Army Painter Strong Tone

5 Buff drybrush

If you wish to add further texture and detail to your netting, you can give it a gentle drybrush with a buff tone. As the model is already painted, I will use a smaller drybrush, and concentrate the effect into the centre of the net, aiming to keep it away from the edges. Once this is completed, the netting is finished

Brush used	Paint
Size 4 flat	Vallejo 976 Buff

10

Winter Camouflage

Winter camouflage is a very evocative way to create an impressive looking model. The way the white paint contrasts with the underlying camouflage can look particularly good, although this can be somewhat tricky to achieve.

During the Second World War, as inclement weather came in, winter whitewash was issued across the combatants to help disguise the vehicles and could be easily removed once the snow had gone.

The whitewash would be applied by crews or maintenance units, often in a hurry, and either painted by hand or sprayed on. In some instances, it was applied by broom and mop. As a result, the finish would often be somewhat rough. This roughness was further exacerbated by the process of the crew moving around the vehicle, as well as the effects of weather.

This combination of rushed application, temporary paint and general wear and tear in harsh weather conditions led to all levels of damage to the paint. Some vehicles may appear mostly white, whilst others can been seen with only traces of white in the more protected areas. Replicating this level of distress can be achieved with a few simple techniques, via an airbrush, rattle can or brush. All of these methods are best used over a basic version of your particular nation's standard colours. An Olive Drab or Dark Green aerosol can will be a great way to begin painting Allied vehicles, whilst a Sand base, and simply applied camouflage pattern will work well on German vehicles.

Depending on the colour scheme you are representing, it may be worth adding the transfers at this stage, as often the vehicle's existing markings would be painted over and around when the white paint was applied.

Do not do any weathering before applying the whitewash effects, although once the whitewash is on, you can use any of the weathering methods as well as the techniques for applying washes as detailed in the various national guides. All of them will work well with a whitewash effect.

BRUSH METHOD

This is by far the simplest method to apply to a model and will give you a finish very close to a freshly painted vehicle. We will simply brush paint the vehicle with white paint over some green applied from an aerosol can.

Using an older size 2 brush, I've thinned the white paint a little, and applied it keeping the brush moving in a vertical direction, working methodically along each surface of the vehicle. Be careful not to overload the brush, as you want to get an even layer of paint across the model without it pooling into the recesses.

With the whitewash applied, you can weather it as detailed elsewhere in this book. You do not need to add a protective varnish or clear coat.

Brush used	Paint
Old size 2 round	AK 11001 White

SPONGE METHOD

In some ways, this method is very similar to the brush technique, but this time we are aiming for a rougher, more heavily worn effect to the paint. We will use a piece of packing sponge to stipple white paint over the base tone of the model, and then to further enhance the weathering, stipple on the base tone of your nation's vehicle to give an effect of heavy wear.

It's worth noting that you can also sponge on the base tone with any of the other methods of whitewash to further enhance any wear and tear present on the vehicle.

1 Sponge on white

Firstly, prepare some paint on a palette. Thin it a little from the pot so that it is not too thick, dab the sponge into the paint, remove the excess

on some kitchen paper, and then with a jabbing motion, use the sponge to build up the opacity of the white paint on the surface of the vehicle.

Brush used	Paint
Packing sponge or foam	AK 11001 White

2 Sponge on base tone

As this is a German vehicle, I will use a Dunkelgelb colour to chip the model. Using the same techniques, apply paint to a palette, load up the sponge, remove excess paint by dabbing it onto some kitchen paper, and then stipple the green paint around the edges of the hull, hatches and any surfaces liable to heavy erosion. You will not need to clear coat the model and can now proceed to weather it.

Brush used	Paint
Size 4 round, make-up brush	AK 11318 Dunkelgelb

CHIPPING FLUID

The final method is one that has gained much popularity in the last decade or so for applying damaged whitewash to a model. After priming the model with the underlying paint colour, apply a layer of chipping fluid, let this set until it is touch-dry and then apply the white paint. This is a more airbrush intensive method, but there are ways around this, which will be covered as we go.

I Spray with chipping fluid.

With the vehicle painted green, we will give it a layer of chipping fluid. There are many of these on the market, and they are best applied with an airbrush, in a few passes to build up a solid layer. It should take around twenty to thirty minutes to be touch-dry and ready to move on to the next stage.

If you do not own an airbrush, you can achieve a similar effect with hairspray. The main difference between the two is that the hairspray will spray on thicker, which will mean that removing the white paint will be less controlled.

Both of these products can be reactivated with water and are an excellent way of applying chipping to a painted surface.

Brush used	Product
Sparmax Max-4	AK 089 Heavy Chipping fluid

2 Spray white

The next step is to mist on some white paint using an airbrush. Apply it in fairly thin layers and gradually let the opacity build up. You want to have the paint thin and even to avoid any pooling.

If you do not own an airbrush, you can instead use an aerosol white paint. I would not suggest using a brush to apply the white, however, as this could reactivate the chipping fluid/hairspray layer and harm the chipping effect.

Brush used	Paint
Sparmax Max-4	AK 11001 White

3 Chip the paint

Leave the paint to set until it is touch-dry. This will vary depending on the particular paint brand you are using, as well as what thinning mediums you have, so it is worth a little experimenting first.

To reactivate the chipping medium, you will need to apply some warm water, paint it onto the surface of the model, leave it for a few minutes, and then gently scrub the areas you want to remove paint from with an old brush. You should begin to see the white paint peeling off to reveal the underlying colours. If you want more precision, you can also use a cocktail stick to add further scratches to the paint. This is also a good way to scratch the paint in smaller, more controlled areas such as around hatches.

Once you are happy with the finish on the model, leave it to dry overnight and then seal the finish with some matt varnish. This will prevent the paint from reactivating when you go on to do further weathering.

Brush used	Paint
Sparmax Max-4	Windsor & Newton Galeria matt

Dear Reader,

We hope you have enjoyed this book, but why not share your views on social media? You can also follow our pages to see more about our other products: facebook.com/penandswordbooks or follow us on Twitter @penswordbooks

You can also view our products at www.pen-and-sword.co.uk (UK and ROW) or www.penandswordbooks.com (North America).

To keep up to date with our latest releases and online catalogues, please sign up to our newsletter at: www.pen-and-sword.co.uk/newsletter

If you would like a printed catalogue with our latest books, then please email: enquiries@pen-and-sword.co.uk or telephone: 01226 734555 (UK and ROW) or email: Uspen-and-sword@casematepublishers.com or telephone: (610) 853-9131 (North America).

We respect your privacy and we will only use personal information to send you information about our products.

Thank you!